THE

Cupcake Café

COOKBOOK

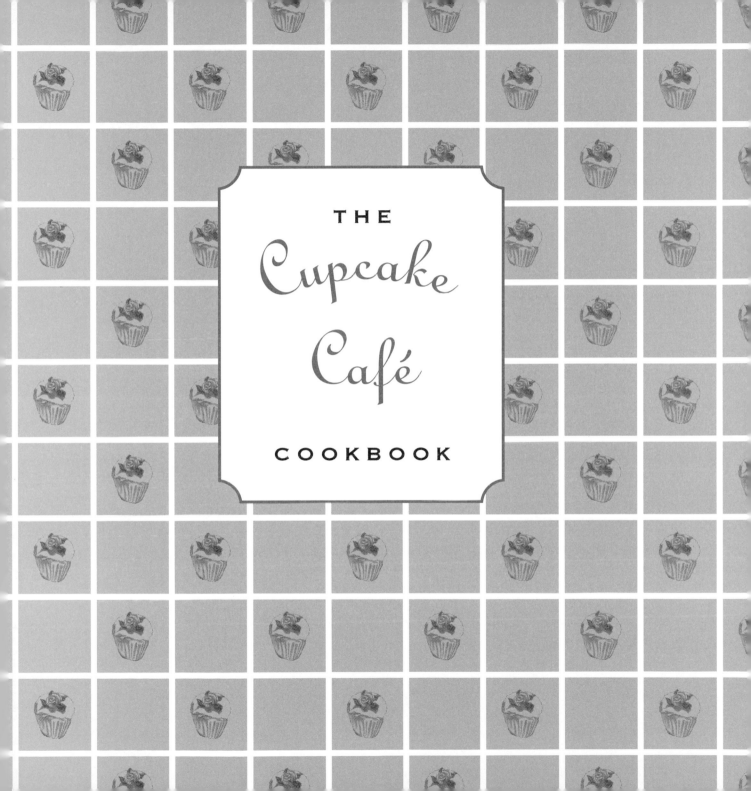

THE
Cupcake
Café
COOKBOOK

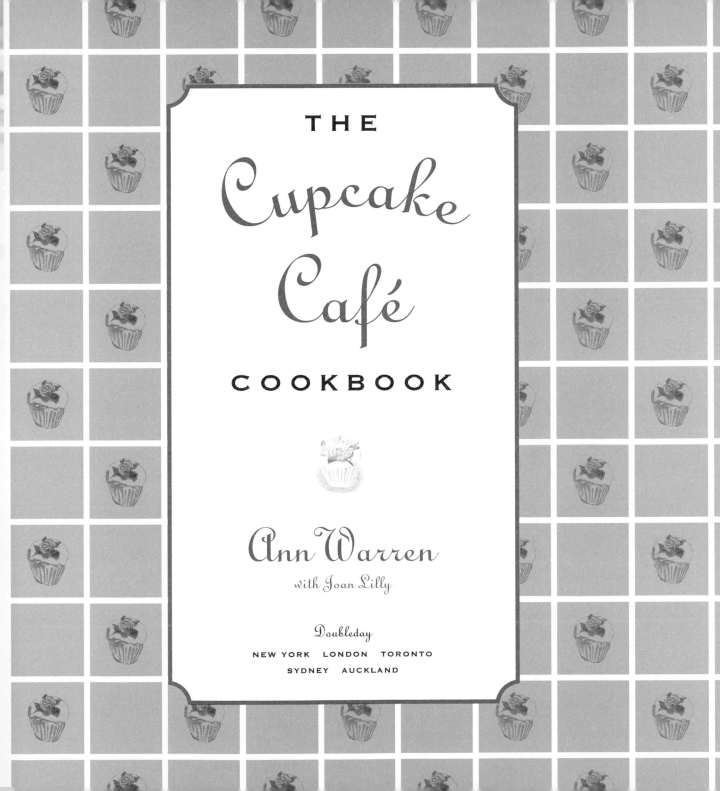

Ann Warren

with *Joan Lilly*

Doubleday

NEW YORK LONDON TORONTO
SYDNEY AUCKLAND

Published by Doubleday
a division of Bantam Doubleday Dell Publishing Group, Inc.
1540 Broadway, New York, New York 10036

Doubleday and the portrayal of an anchor with a dolphin are
trademarks of Doubleday, a division of Bantam Doubleday Dell
Publishing Group, Inc.

Book design by Jennifer Ann Daddio

The recipe for Whole Wheat Orange Doughnuts on page 33
is reprinted with the permission of *Gourmet* magazine.

Library of Congress Cataloging-in-Publication Data
Warren, Ann.
The Cupcake Café cookbook/Ann Warren with Joan Lilly.
—1st ed.
p.   cm.
1. Baking. 2. Baked products. 3. Cupcake Café. I. Lilly, Joan.
II. Cupcake Café. III. Title.
TX765.W34   1998
641.8'15—dc21   97-52726

CIP

ISBN 0-385-48339-2
Printed in the United States of America
August 1998
First Edition
1   3   5   7   9   10   8   6   4   2

In memory of our father Scott B. Lilly,
who always encouraged artistic endeavors.

Acknowledgments

I would like to thank first my sister Joan, without whose help this book would not exist; my editor Judith Kern; Rachel Dinnerstein, Cynthia Fairbanks, Jason Harrison, Nora Byron, Jose Martinez, Hermelindo Ortega, Rick Estrin, Edward Cohen, and Brian Lynch for contributions of time, art, and recipe testing; my daughter Jane, who endured this project for what must have seemed forever; and my husband Michael, who wanted to have me committed when it was first suggested, but didn't; and to all our patient customers, who have ever waited without complaint for their cake.

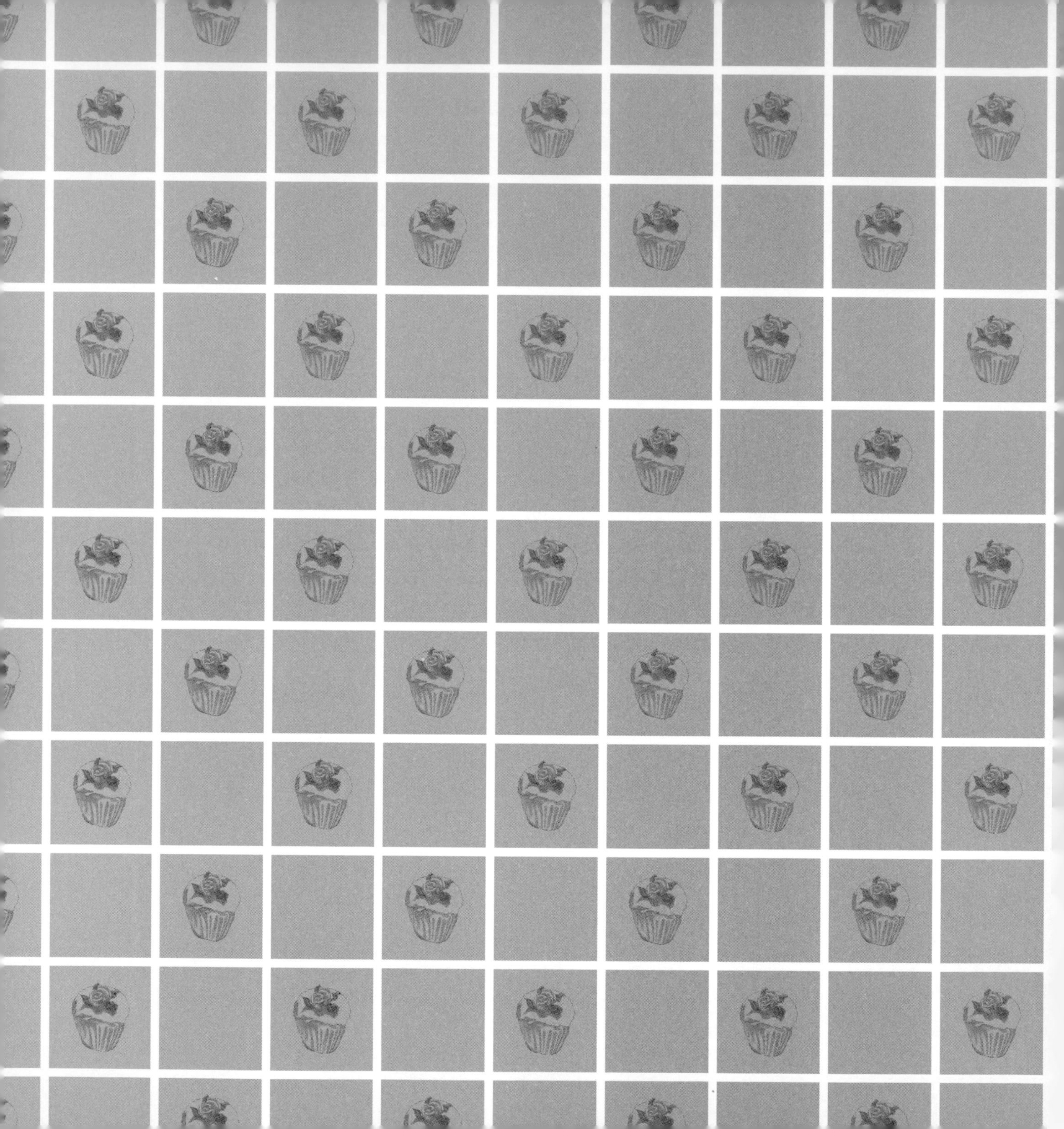

Contents

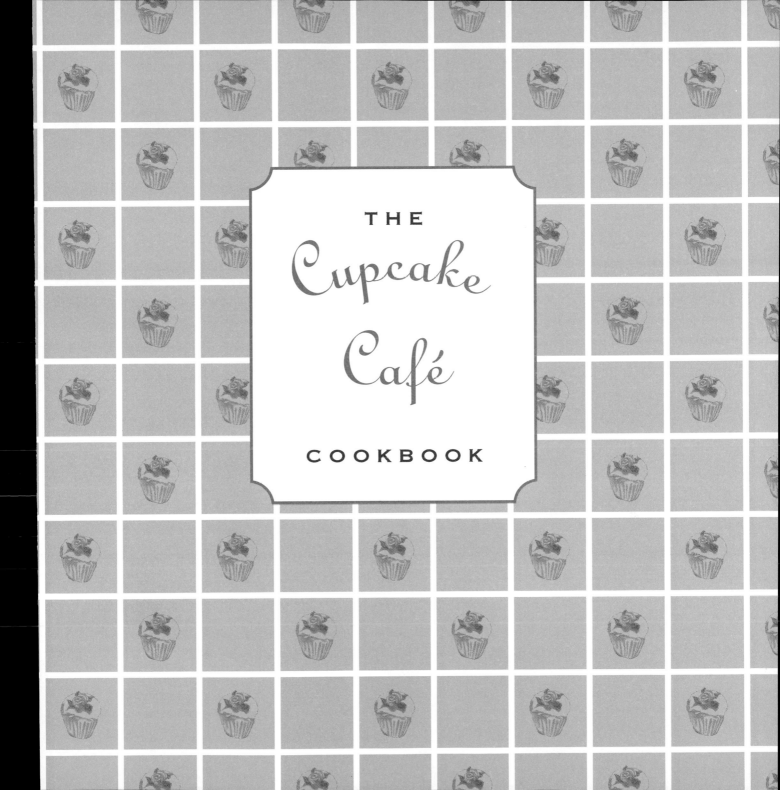

THE

Cupcake
Café

COOKBOOK

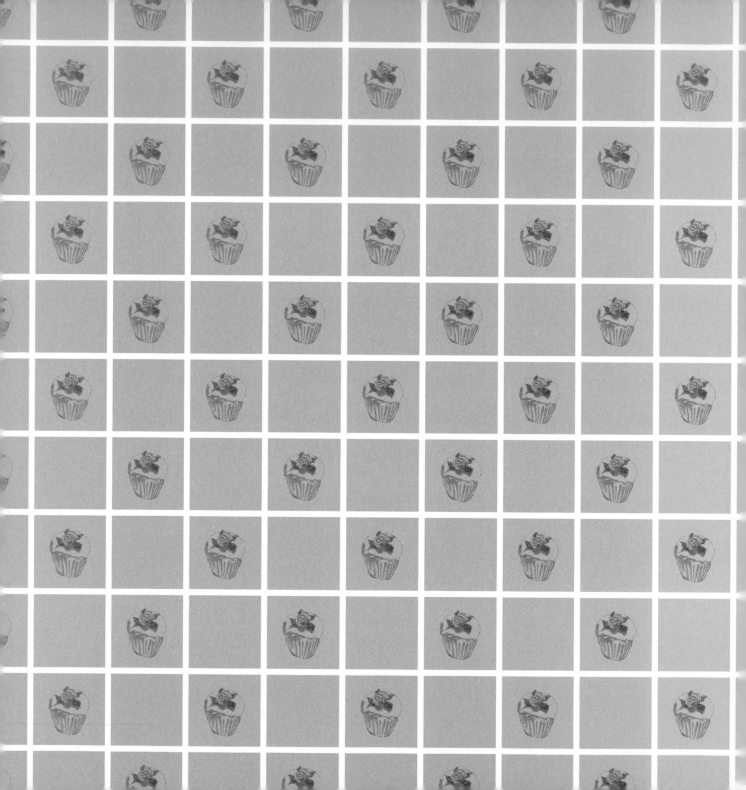

Introduction

BY JOAN LILLY

Some History

Ann and Michael Warren opened the Cupcake Café in the spring of 1988 on the corner of Ninth Avenue and Thirty-ninth Street in Manhattan's Hell's Kitchen (the neighborhood also known, less evocatively, as Clinton), the former stomping grounds—literally—of the Westies, an Irish gang infamous for the inconsiderate things they used to do to people in bathtubs.

Another bakery had occupied the corner storefront before the Cupcake, and because I lived up the block, and at the time the only other very-local shopping options were illegal substances and transvestites who were much too tall for me, I used to go there regularly. The bakery's entire selection appeared to consist of two or three kinds of cookies, Italian bread, and, in the summer, ices. I always bought quarter-pound bags of Regina biscuits—those thumb-sized hard cookies coated in sesame seeds. The proprietor was an elderly woman of considerable size and minimal conversation, who seemed to spend the entire day leaning against the counter, arms folded in front of her, baseball bat at her side. For some reason the lights were always off. During the summer, the darkness lent the place a sort of soothing coolness. Most of the time it just made it hard to see.

Michael and Ann had been scouting around for a spot to open a wholesale doughnut operation. Michael had finished about ten years at the Well-Bred Loaf, clomping around covered in flour (where he met Ann, who worked part-time slicing her fingers on brownie tins so that she could paint), and they'd decided to venture out on their own. I will resist the cute anecdote about early Ann standing on a box to stir something on the stove; suffice it to say Ann has been cooking and baking seriously forever.

When she called and told me that she and Michael had rented the bakery down the street from me, I had an intimation that I'd end up working there. Soon I was standing behind the same counter as my taciturn predecessor, selling muffins, scones, coffee cakes, sticky buns, doughnuts, and for those who know how to start the day off right, delicious fruit pies—all made on the premises. Nothing fancy, but all very tasty and reassuring. (The retired former proprietor left her bat, which still inspires seasonal talk of a Cupcake Café softball team.)

Ann and Michael didn't undertake a major renovation before opening. They just removed some paint from the marble walls and turned on the lights. So it shouldn't have come as a surprise that some of the customers of the old bakery didn't immediately grasp that a change in ownership had occurred. During the Cupcake's first days in business, when customers were scarce, men in Damon Runyonesque attire would appear in the doorway on a regular basis and, in a state of disorientation (What were the lights doing on?), inquire about buying their daily number. Usually something—probably the absurd pleated stovepipe chef's hats we original counter people wore—tipped them off to the possibility that they were now in the wrong place, and they would seamlessly switch their order to fresh yeast (which, for the record, the Cupcake also doesn't sell).

Why Ann, who is essentially a morning toast eater, and Michael, who, if anyone were keeping track, would probably qualify for a regional oatmeal consumption award, decided to open a place whose original mission was to offer made-from-scratch doughnuts, remains something of a mystery. Perhaps they were motivated in part by a sense of history—New York's original doughnut-frying establishment had been located within blocks of the Cupcake—and a concern that the tradition of fresh doughnuts in New York not be allowed to fade. What is clear is that, while the doughnuts continue to win recognition and have retained their place of honor in the Cupcake's offerings, it is the decorated cakes that have made it difficult to find anyone in several states who has not heard of the place. Despite the fact that the only advertising the Cupcake has ever taken out was in a children's magazine called *Zuzu,* overnight (one of those long nights that takes about two years) Ann went from decorating cakes with portraits of dearly departed German shepherds to decorating birthday cakes for Madonna and Mick Jagger.

Our friend Ed Cohen attributes the Cupcake's appeal to its time-warp ambiance. What with the 1920s and 1930s music, and the resistance-to-renovation interior, you might easily think you were walking into a 1940s coffee shop, were it not for the stray purple- or green-haired counter person. However, I'm more inclined to think that the Café's appeal comes from the fact that people have adopted it as a second home, one that's a bit more chaotic than their own perhaps, but where they feel equally comfortable and can count on there always being something good to eat. When she was about three, Ann's and Michael's daughter, Jane, asked whether she lived at the Cupcake. For a lot of our neighbors, the Cupcake is at least an added room.

The Book

The Cupcake Café Cookbook includes recipes for all the baked goods sold in the Café scaled down to household proportions and capable of being created without either elaborate equipment or very much in the way of baking experience. We didn't include any of the Café's "real food" offerings (quiche, soup, sandwiches, and the like) and make no promises about a sequel, so you'll just have to keep having lunch out.

The majority of the book, though, is about cakes: baking, basting, decorating, inscribing, and even constructing (as in multitiered layer cakes). If this volume is discovered on your shelves, you may suddenly find yourself bamboozled into doing all your friends' wedding cakes. Ann goes beyond how to keep your butter cream roses from looking like radiated cabbages, and includes thoughts on color and design. She also covers what we call "picture cakes"—how to paint illustrations on cakes—and offers ideas for children's cakes. So go forth, make your cake, and admire it, too.

Doughnuts

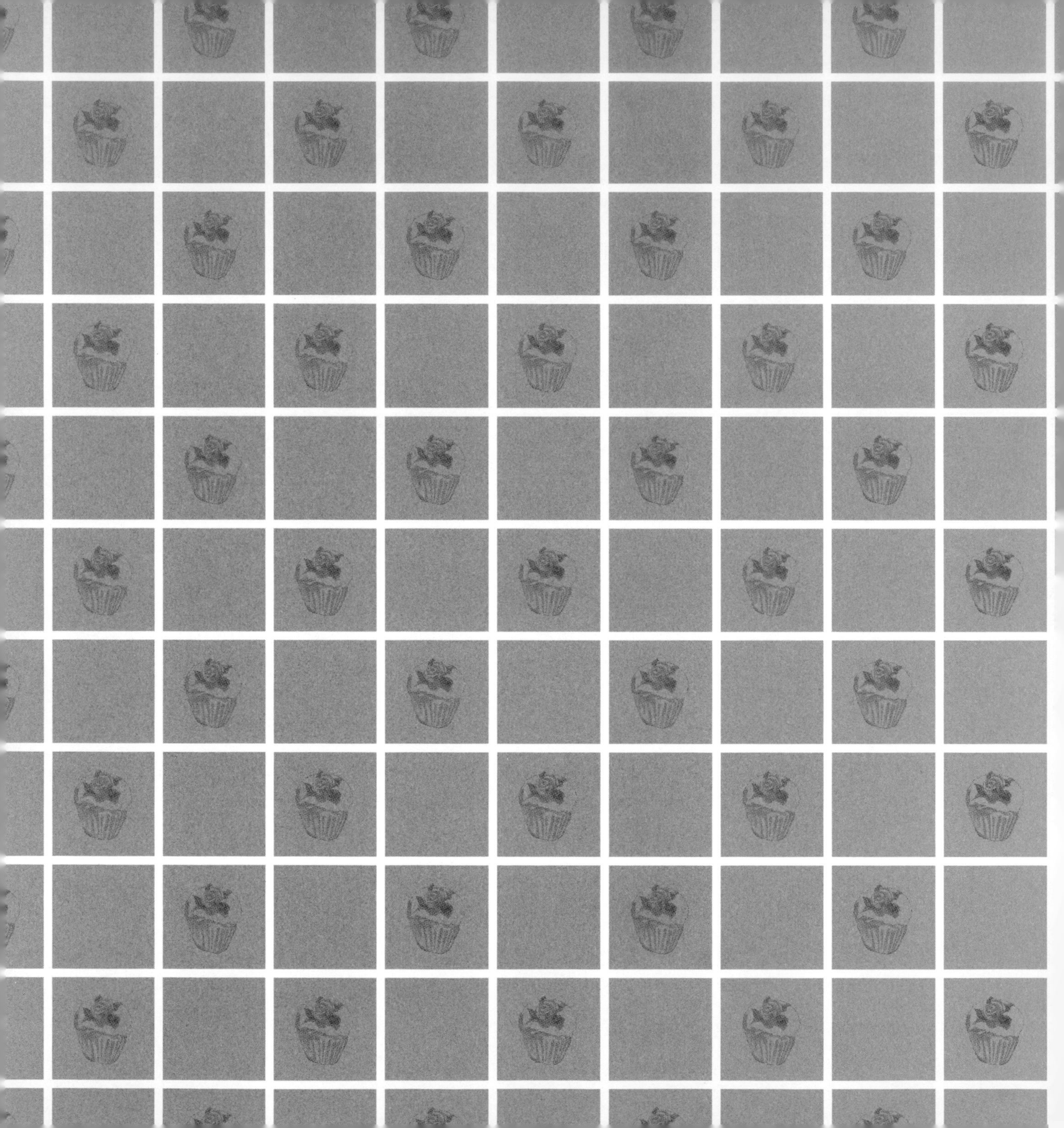

*I*f you have never made doughnuts at home, you should. While there are places in the world where homemade doughnuts are pretty common, if it is not your lot to live in such a place, and the only way you are going to experience homemade doughnuts is to open your own home to this enterprise, do not be daunted! A warm, fresh, chemically untainted doughnut is something to be experienced at least once.

In truth, even a mediocre doughnut is pretty good as long as it's still warm. For years, the main attraction for Michael and me at the Kimberton Fair in rural Pennsylvania was the wonderful doughnuts we consumed by the greasy bagful. When we finally made discreet inquiries among members of the Volunteer Fire Company Ladies' Auxiliary—the doughnut-makers at the fairground—we learned that they worked from a bulk commercial mix, and so we had to attribute the greater part of those doughnuts' charm to their warmth and freshness.

I could try to sell you on this enterprise by implying that, as a badge of old-fashioned domesticity, home doughnut-frying is likely to lead to marriage and children. But I realize that for some this may be a deterrent. So rather than frightening you with images of barn raisings, church suppers, and warm cozy rural kitchens, I suggest you imagine the trenches of World War I, the Salvation Army, Times Square (where the first automated doughnut machine was used), and Edward Hopper's *Night Hawks*.

Why Doughnuts Aren't Really So Bad for You

Some of you might have other reservations about making a couple of dozen doughnuts—reservations related to the possibility of eating even a *small* portion of a couple of dozen doughnuts. In the Age of Reason most people would not even consider allowing dozens of doughnuts into their home. Lucky for us the Age of Reason occurred nearly 200 years ago, and we can now eat all the doughnuts we want!

If this logic hasn't moved you, go on to my fragile argument for doughnuts as a health food: To fry properly, doughnut batter can be neither too sweet nor too rich. All that sugary stuff is added *after* the doughnut is fried, and you don't have to add it at all. And while I grant there is no getting around the fact that a doughnut is a fried food, it is also true that, once fried, the damage stops—few doughnut eaters put butter or cream cheese on their doughnuts.

Further to my doughnuts-as-health-food argument: A doughnut does not have to include any strange chemicals. A doughnut can include whole wheat flour, wheat germ, oats, powdered skim milk, egg whites, fruit, and ground nuts.

The doughnut recipes included here are the same as those we use at the Cupcake Café, which means they are free of chemicals and are made entirely from scratch (for example, we use real potatoes, not dried flakes). Even without preservatives, they should taste quite good for at least a day, and a good deal longer if you freeze them. Frozen doughnuts can be revived in a toaster oven. Give them about 7 minutes at 300°F if straight from the freezer, less if you've let them defrost a bit. When you take them out of the oven, place them on paper towels to absorb the reactivated oil.

To make doughnuts at home is to unravel a great culinary mystery. Just invite enough people over when you make them or have somewhere in mind to take them (the freezer could qualify here as "somewhere") so that you personally are not obliged to consume the entire batch.

Now that we've worked up some enthusiasm for this project, I'll discuss equipment and all the things that can go wrong.

Equipment

For any of these doughnut recipes you will need something in which to fry the doughnuts. Several things will work well, and quite a few seemingly suitable items won't. I personally have destroyed a great deal of cookware figuring this out, and I don't see why you should have to go through the same ordeal.

Suitable items for frying doughnuts at home:

1. A deep, cast-iron, flat-bottom kettle that is *pure* cast iron
2. An electric fryer at least 5 inches deep

Unsuitable for frying doughnuts:

1. Enameled pots (including Le Creuset)—interesting and horrible things happen to enameled pots, rendering the post-frying pot unsuitable for any purpose thereafter.
2. Any pot with a non-stick coating (weird peeling can occur)
3. Any pot too shallow—which means less than 5 inches; this is to avoid fat-spilling and grease fires. (To be on the safe side 6 inches wouldn't hurt.)

Here, courtesy of Belshaw Brothers, is a chart listing all the things that can possibly go wrong while frying. This is to impress you so that you'll take the whole thing seriously and be plenty proud of yourself when everything works out.

1. What is the correct dough temperature?

Between 75° and 80°F. Regulate by using water of proper temperature.

2. What happens if the dough is too warm?

The donuts will lack volume, may be misshapen.

3. *What happens if the dough is too cold?*

The donuts stay under the fat too long; they fry too slowly and tend either to crack open or to form ball donuts, absorb excess fat and lose volume.

4. *Why is a floor time recommended?*

A 10 to 15 minute rest period between mixing and cutting permits the dry ingredients to take up the water and helps produce donuts of good volume and proper fat penetration.

5. *What happens if the floor time is too long?*

There are no ill effects unless it is extended beyond 30 minutes.

6. *What happens if the floor time is too short?*

The donuts will have less volume than they should and may be slightly tough.

7. *What is the correct fat temperature for frying?*

Best results usually are obtained at from 370° to 380°.

8. *What happens if the fat temperature is too high?*

The donut fries too fast on the outside, proper expansion is prevented, volume will be subnormal, and the interior crumb may be close. In extreme cases, the centers may be raw.

9. *What happens if the fat temperature is too low?*

The donut spreads too rapidly, forms large rings, and tends to crack open. The crust color will be light and the fat absorption high.

10. *What happens when the fat level is too far below the cutter?*

Donuts are apt to turn over while submerging or surfacing. This may produce cracked or rough crusted donuts.

11. How far should the frying screen be below the fat surface?

The best distance is from 2 to 3 inches while the dough is being dropped. The distance should be adjusted so that the donuts rise with the top side up just as the dough came from the cutter. Most frying kettles are from 6″ to 8″ deep — put screen in to reduce depth of grease.

12. What happens when the screen is too near the surface?

The dough may stick on the screen and delay in rising. This in turn may result in a heavily crusted or cracked donut, low in volume, and screen marked.

13. What happens when the screen is too deep in the fat?

The donut frequently turns over while rising. Cracked and crippled donuts nearly always result.

14. How can donuts be prevented from sticking to the drainer screens in open kettle frying?

Keep the drainer screens clean so that donuts will break away quickly and rise promptly to the surface. Clean carbonized or dirty screens with a wire brush and a mild solution of hot washing soda to remove all adhering material to which the dough will stick.

15. Can fat absorption be too low?

Yes. Fat absorption can be too low and may result in donuts with poor keeping qualities. Donuts probably should absorb between 1½ and 3 ounces of frying fat per dozen depending on their weight.

16. How can excessive fat absorption be prevented?

Excessive fat absorption may be reduced by: giving a floor time, mixing the dough a little longer than usual, having the dough at the proper temperature, having the frying fat at the proper temperature, and turning the donut promptly when they have taken on a golden brown color. Do not overfry them on the first side.

There are two basic categories of doughnut—yeast and cake. Yeast doughnuts are the fluffier kind (the sort that you can pull apart, like glazed and jelly doughnuts). Cake doughnuts are the sort you can break rather than pull, the standard dunking doughnut. I'll start with yeast doughnuts.

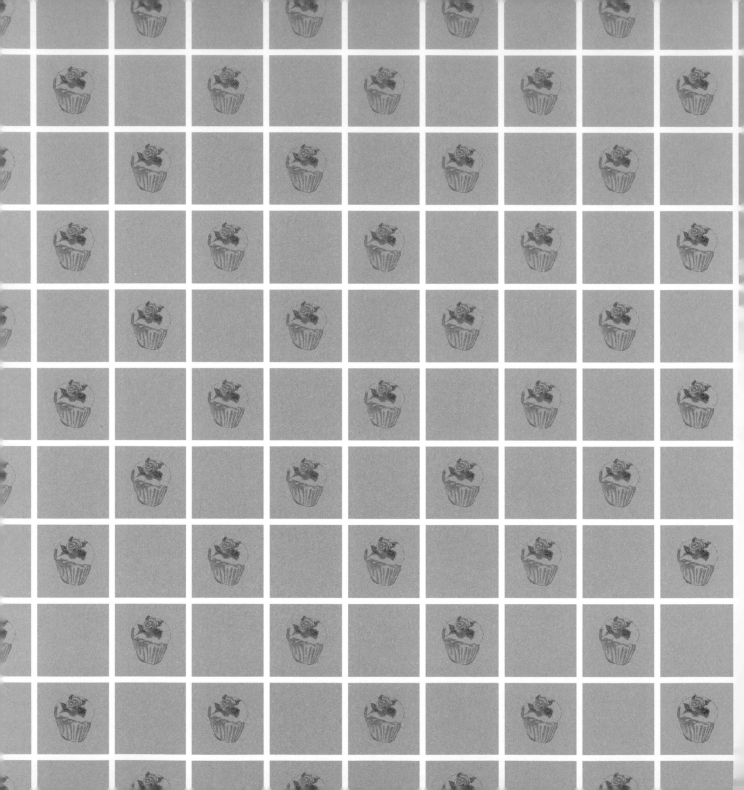

Jelly Doughnuts

*Probably the best thing about making your own jelly doughnuts is being able to
fill them with whatever jam or preserves you choose, and with as much as you want. Of course there are
some physical restraints here, particularly if you fill the doughnuts before you fry them, which is
the more common method when making them at home. It's faster to fill them after they've been fried, but
if the jelly is already in when the frying happens, its sweet fruit flavor will suffuse the delicate
flesh of the doughnut. Since jelly doughnuts are made with a yeast dough, you need to allow enough time
for them to rise twice before frying. If you are planning a morning fry, make the dough
the night before and refrigerate it.*

2 OUNCES FRESH CAKE YEAST

½ CUP TEPID WATER (95° TO 100°F)

1 TEASPOON GRANULATED SUGAR

¼ CUP DARK BROWN SUGAR

3 EGGS PLUS 1 EXTRA YOLK

½ CUP COOKED AND RICED POTATOES
    (ABOUT 2 MEDIUM POTATOES)

6 OUNCES BUTTER, MELTED (¾ CUP)

1 CUP SCALDED MILK

1 TEASPOON FRESH GRATED LEMON
    RIND

1 TEASPOON PURE VANILLA EXTRACT

4 CUPS ALL-PURPOSE FLOUR, PLUS
    ADDITIONAL AS NEEDED

1 TEASPOON SALT

½ TEASPOON BAKING POWDER

2 TABLESPOONS DRY POWDERED MILK

1 EGG WHITE MIXED WITH ½ CUP MILK

8–12 OUNCES JELLY

SOLID VEGETABLE SHORTENING
    (USE APPROXIMATELY ¾ POUND
    SHORTENING PER QUART OF FRYER
    CAPACITY—FOR A 4-QUART VESSEL,
    USE ABOUT 3 POUNDS SHORTENING)

POWDERED SUGAR, FOR DUSTING
    (OPTIONAL)

Mix the yeast with the warm water and granulated sugar and set aside for 5 minutes. Watch to see that the yeast foams before adding it to the other ingredients.

Mix the brown sugar, whole eggs, and extra yolk together. Add the riced potatoes, melted butter, and scalded milk and stir. Add the lemon rind and vanilla. Sift the flour. Stir the salt, baking powder, and dry milk into the flour.

Add the proofed yeast to the wet ingredients and mix well. Add all the flour, adding more flour if is too sticky or wet. Knead like a bread dough for about 5 minutes. Allow the dough to rise until doubled in bulk, then knead again. Roll it out to about $1/4$ inch thick and cut the dough into circles. Use a biscuit cutter, a cookie cutter, or the rim of a glass about $2^1/2$ to 3 inches in diameter. Brush the edges of the circles with the egg and milk mixture. This is your egg wash. If you are filling the doughnuts now, take about a tablespoon of jam, jelly, or preserves and spoon it onto the center of half of the circles. Cover each of these circles with one of the circles without jam (sandwich-style), egg wash side down. Press firmly around the edges to seal in the jam or jelly. Try not to get any jam over the seal or on the outside of the doughnut, where it would burn.

Allow the doughnuts to rise again, about 45 minutes. The length of time it will take for a yeast dough to rise depends in part on the surrounding temperature. Times are given for "room temperature" assuming a normal room temperature. (So if it's midsummer and you don't have an air conditioner, take that into account.) Dough will rise faster in a warmer spot, but a short rising time is not always desirable for flavor, or even necessarily convenient. Even in a relatively cold spot, such as a refrigerator, yeast dough will rise, albeit quite slowly. This "retarding" of the dough can allow you to prepare doughnut dough the night before and fry them in the morning. A longer rise will impart a nice yeast flavor. In a refrigerator a doubling in bulk should take about five to eight hours—longer for the first rising, shorter for a second. Wherever your dough is rising, do not try to speed things along by allowing your dough to get too warm. Too much heat can kill the yeast and even prematurely cook part of your dough. If you wish to fill the doughnuts after they are fried, form the doughnuts without jam inside but sealed the same way—seal two circles together and allow to rise again.

Near the end of the rising time, gradually heat your frying shortening to 365°F. Shortening that is too hot will brown the doughnuts too quickly. Shortening that is not hot enough can result in greasy doughnuts. Fry the doughnuts by lowering them carefully into the shortening with a slotted spoon. Leave room for your doughnuts to expand a little. And don't put in too many doughnuts at once, as this may drastically lower the temperature of the shortening. Unless you are using an electric fryer with a thermostat, keep close watch on the temperature and adjust it accordingly. Fry the doughnuts about 30 seconds, then turn over one doughnut. If brown, turn over the others with a slotted spoon. Depending on your fryer, each side will take ½ minute to 1½ minutes. Allow them another 30 seconds to 1½ minutes on the other side and remove. Drain these on paper towels and continue to fry the rest of your doughnut circles.

When cool enough to handle, unfilled doughnuts can be filled. Put whatever jam, jelly, or preserve you have chosen into a pastry bag with a #230 nozzle attached, or a #7 tip. Push the jam-filled tip into a doughnut (you'll find the nozzle is a better tool here) and give the bag a good squeeze.

Cooled doughnuts can be dusted with powdered sugar, if you wish.

MAKES ABOUT 2 DOZEN DOUGHNUTS

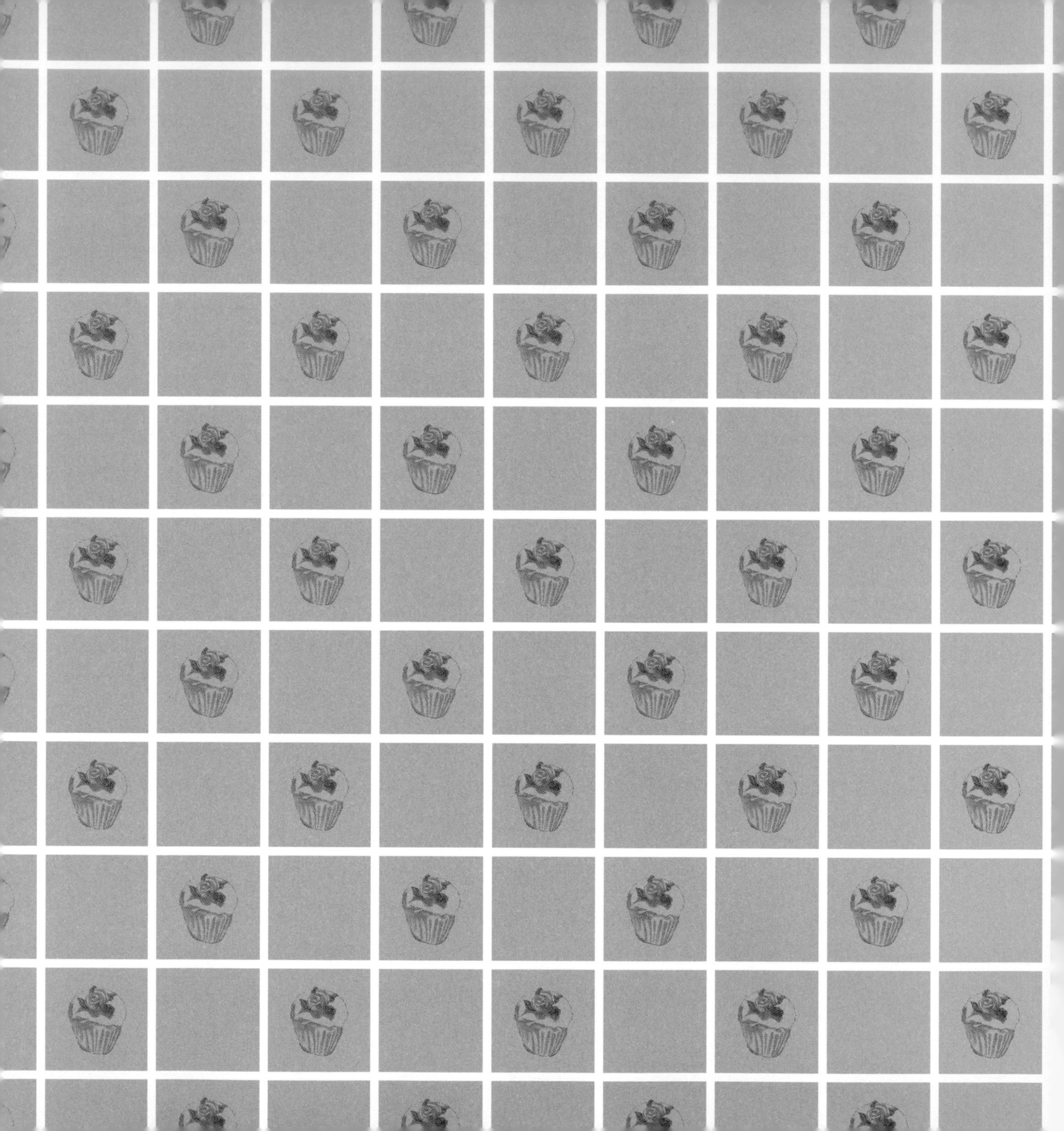

Glazed Doughnuts

*Both these glazed doughnut recipes have potato in them and keep well until
the next day. These are yeast doughnuts, so allow time for them to rise twice. I prefer them with no
glaze at all (a little granulated sugar is nice), but I've put personal preference aside
and include the recipe for glaze here as well.*

1 ½ OUNCES FRESH CAKE YEAST

1 CUP TEPID WATER (95° TO 100°F)

1 TEASPOON SUGAR

¼ POUND BUTTER

1 CUP SCALDED MILK

¾ CUP COOKED AND RICED POTATO (2
TO 3 POTATOES, DEPENDING ON SIZE)

¾ CUP LIGHT BROWN SUGAR

2 EGGS PLUS 2 EXTRA YOLKS

1 ¼ TEASPOONS PURE VANILLA
EXTRACT

¼ TEASPOON LEMON OIL

2 ⅓ CUPS DRY POWDERED MILK

1 TEASPOON BAKING POWDER

¼ TEASPOON BAKING SODA

¾ TEASPOON SALT

¼ CUP OAT FLOUR (FINELY GROUND
OATMEAL ALSO WORKS)

6 CUPS UNBLEACHED FLOUR, PLUS
ADDITIONAL AS NEEDED

1 RECIPE GLAZE (FOLLOWS)

3 POUNDS VEGETABLE SHORTENING
(SUCH AS CRISCO) FOR A 4-QUART
FRYER (OR ¾ POUND PER QUART
CAPACITY)

Proof the yeast in 1 cup water with 1 teaspoon sugar (that is, "prove" that the yeast is still alive by allowing it to stand for 5 to 7 minutes, checking that it foams before adding it to the other ingredients). Add the butter to the scalded milk. Add the potato, brown sugar, eggs, egg yolks, vanilla, and lemon oil. Mix together the powdered milk, baking powder, soda, salt, oat flour, and unbleached flour. Add the proofed yeast mix to the mix you've made with the milk, eggs, potato, etc. Add the flour mix to this. Knead, adding more flour if needed to form a dough that can be rolled out. Allow the dough to rise until doubled, about 45 minutes to 1 hour, then knead it again. The length of time it will take for a yeast dough to rise depends in part on the surrounding temperature. Times are given for "room temperature" assuming a normal room temperature. (So if it's midsummer and you don't have an air conditioner, take that into account.) Dough will rise faster in a warmer spot, but a short rising time is not always desirable for flavor, or even necessarily convenient. Even in a relatively cold spot, such as a refrigerator, yeast dough will rise, albeit quite slowly. This "retarding" of the dough can allow you to prepare doughnut dough the night before and fry them in the morning. A longer rise will impart a nice yeast flavor. In a refrigerator a doubling in bulk should take about five to eight hours—longer for the first rising, shorter for a second. Wherever your dough is rising, do not try to speed things along by allowing your dough to get too warm. Too much heat can kill the yeast and even prematurely cook part of your dough. Roll out to a 1- to 1½-inch thickness and cut out rings using a doughnut cutter or a larger (3½- to 4-inch) and a smaller (2-inch) biscuit cutter. Gather together the remaining dough and roll it again until all the dough is cut. Allow the cut doughnuts to rise again until doubled in size and then fry, making sure not to fry too many at a time. Fry in a solid vegetable shortening at 370°F about 30 to 45 seconds on each side. Glaze when slightly but not completely cool.

MAKES ABOUT 2½ DOZEN DOUGHNUTS

Glaze

3 CUPS CONFECTIONERS' SUGAR

¼ CUP MAPLE SYRUP

1 TEASPOON HONEY

1 CUP WATER

Combine all the ingredients and either dribble the glaze with a spoon over the slightly cooled doughnuts or dunk them into the glaze—whatever your glaze-to-doughnut ratio preference dictates. Let the glaze set (should take about 10 minutes) before serving.

MAKES ENOUGH FOR ABOUT 2½ DOZEN DOUGHNUTS.

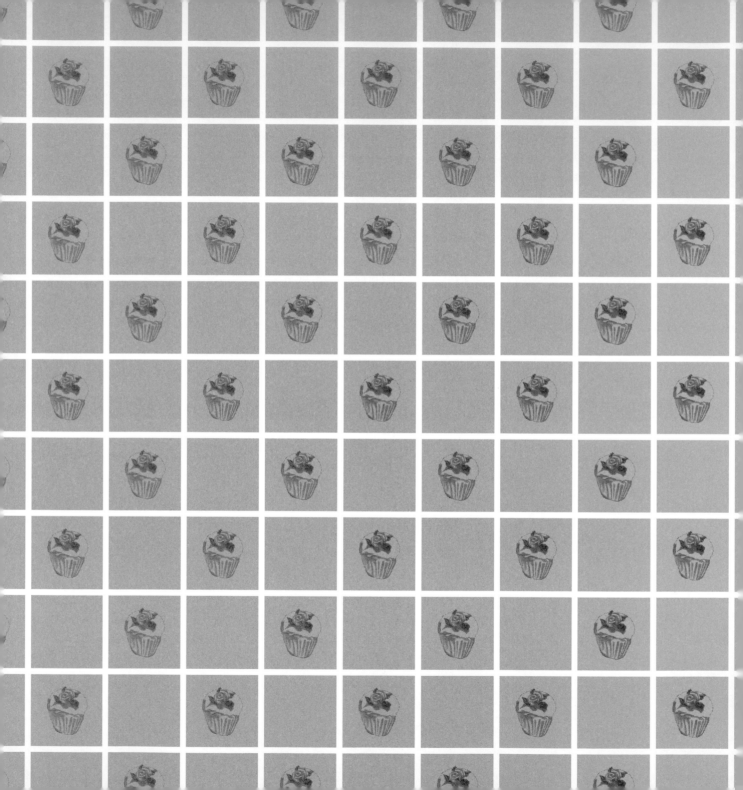

Sweet Potato Glazed Doughnuts

2 OUNCES FRESH CAKE YEAST

½ CUP TEPID WATER (95° TO 100°F),
   PLUS 1 CUP WATER

1 TEASPOON PLUS ½ CUP SUGAR

2 EGGS

4 OUNCES BUTTER, MELTED

1 CUP COOKED AND MASHED SWEET
   POTATO (3 TO 4 POTATOES,
   DEPENDING ON SIZE)

½ TEASPOON GROUND NUTMEG

5 TO 6 CUPS ALL-PURPOSE
   UNBLEACHED FLOUR

SOLID VEGETABLE SHORTENING
   (APPROXIMATELY ¾ POUND PER
   1-QUART FRYER CAPACITY)

1 RECIPE GLAZE (PAGE 21)

Combine the yeast with the ½ cup tepid water and the 1 teaspoon sugar. Let the mixture stand for about 5 minutes, until the yeast foams. Beat together the eggs and the ½ cup sugar. Add the butter and the sweet potato. Add the other cup water. Mix the nutmeg into 4 cups of the flour with the yeast mixture. Knead, adding the rest of the flour as needed to make a workable (i.e., not too sticky) dough similar to the consistency of bread dough.

Preparation is the same for both types of glazed doughnut. Let the dough rise to double in size, then knead again.

Roll the dough out to ¾ to 1 inch thick and cut out rings, using a doughnut cutter or two biscuit cutters, the larger one approximately 2¾ inches, the smaller one approximately 1½ inches. Let the doughnuts rise again until doubled in size. Gradually heat the shortening to 370°F and fry, without overcrowding your kettle or fryer, until browned for about 30 to 45 seconds on each side. (Test one before removing the others.) Drain on absorbent paper. Allow to cool slightly before adding glaze to taste.

MAKES ABOUT 4 DOZEN DOUGHNUTS

CAKE DOUGHNUTS

Cake doughnuts are leavened with baking soda or baking powder rather than with yeast. This means they do not need to be left to rise. The directions given on page 28 for the Dunky Oaty Doughnuts apply to the handling of all the cake doughnuts.

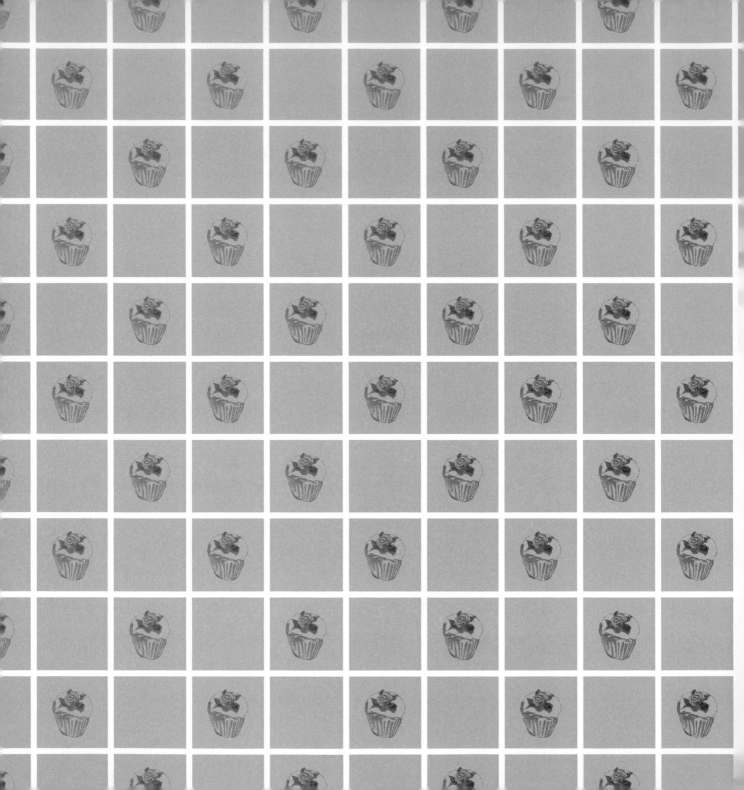

Dunky Oaty Doughnuts

These whole wheat oatmeal doughnuts, which some of our original customers will recall were once sold as "Dunky Oaties," came about because of some insane nostalgia I carried from childhood for Chock full o'Nuts whole wheat doughnuts. I say insane because visits to Chock full o'Nuts were exclusively associated with doctor appointments, so those doughnuts must have been awfully good. We were never able to find a recipe that even remotely resembled Chock full o'Nuts', so we concocted this one; I'm sure the ingredients for this have little in common with their inspiration. These doughnuts are also the closest a doughnut ever comes to being a nutritionally sound investment.

First

2 1/2 CUPS WHOLE WHEAT FLOUR

2 CUPS UNBLEACHED FLOUR

1 TABLESPOON PLUS 1 TEASPOON BAKING POWDER

1 1/2 TEASPOONS BAKING SODA

1 1/3 TEASPOONS SALT

2 TEASPOONS CINNAMON

1/2 TEASPOON MACE

Second

1 CUP CHOPPED WALNUTS (MEDIUM FINE)

1/2 CUP WHEAT GERM

1 2/3 CUP ROLLED OATS

Third

6 EGGS

1 CUP LIGHT BROWN SUGAR

1/3 CUP HONEY

2 OUNCES BUTTER, MELTED (1/4 CUP)

1 TEASPOON GRATED LEMON RIND

2 CUPS BUTTERMILK

3/4 POUND SOLID VEGETABLE SHORTENING PER QUART FRYER CAPACITY (FOR A FOUR-QUART FRYER, USE 3 POUNDS SHORTENING)

POWDERED SUGAR, FOR DUSTING (OPTIONAL)

Sift the first set of ingredients together, then add the second set of ingredients. Combine well and put aside. Combine the third set of ingredients and then add them to the dry mix. Do not overmix. Chill in the refrigerator for between ½ to 1 hour to make handling easier.

When the dough is not too soft or sticky, it is ready to roll out on a floured board. You can use bran or whole wheat flour to flour the board if you like. Roll the dough to ¾ to 1 inch thick and cut rings using a doughnut cutter or two biscuit cutters—first a larger one (about 3 to 2½ inches in diameter), then, inside that, a smaller one (about 1¼ inches). Meanwhile you can be gradually heating up your shortening to about 365°F—not beyond! Fry four or five doughnuts at a time for about 2 minutes on each side. Remove with a long-handled slotted spoon or spatula and place on absorbent paper (such as paper towels) to drain. Continue until all the dough is fried. These can be sprinkled with powdered sugar when cooled slightly.

MAKES ABOUT 1 DOZEN DOUGHNUTS

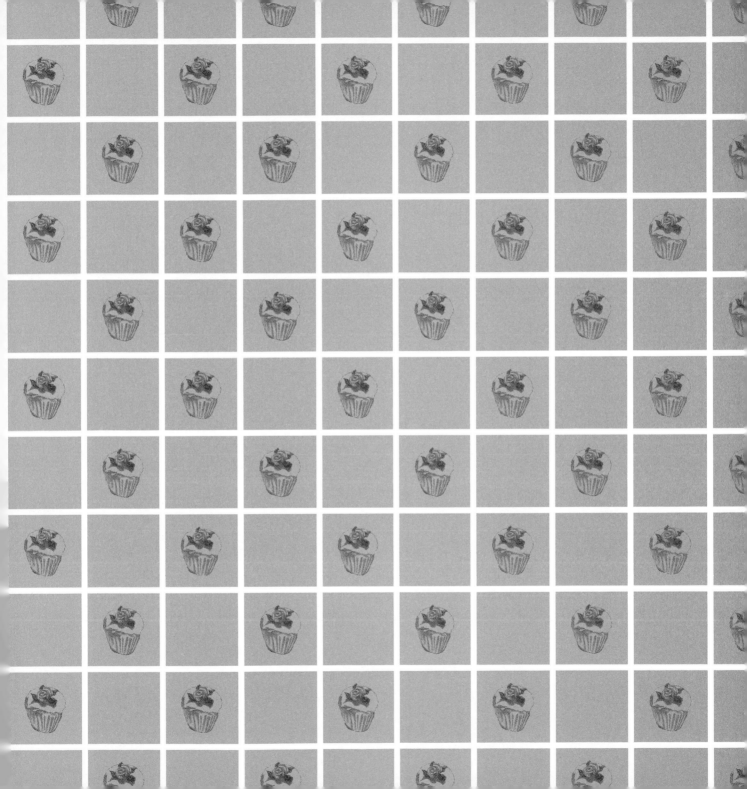

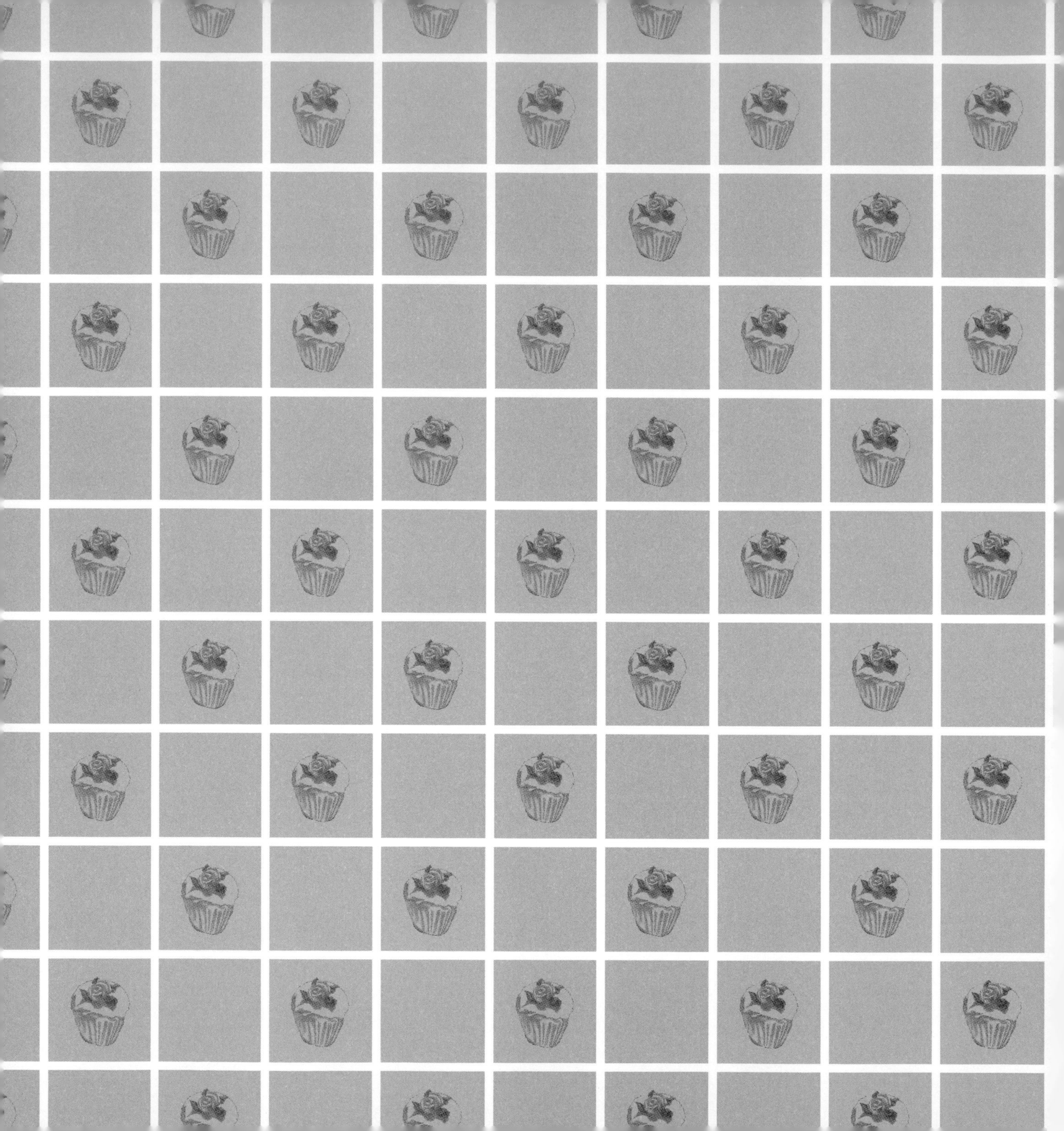

Buttermilk Skies

These are plain vanilla and nutmeg doughnuts similar to, but less rich than Long Island Crullers (page 35). They are tasty and soft.

2½ CUPS PASTRY FLOUR

2½ CUPS ALL-PURPOSE FLOUR

¼ CUP OAT FLOUR (FINELY GROUND OATMEAL ALSO WORKS)

1 TABLESPOON BAKING POWDER

2 TEASPOONS BAKING SODA

½ CUP DRY POWDERED MILK

1½ TEASPOONS GROUND MACE

½ TEASPOON GROUND NUTMEG

⅔ TEASPOON SALT

¾ CUP SUGAR

1½ CUPS COOKED AND RICED POTATOES (4½ TO 6 POTATOES, DEPENDING ON SIZE)

2 TABLESPOONS MELTED BUTTER

3 EGGS PLUS 3 EXTRA YOLKS

2 TABLESPOONS HONEY

½ CUP SOUR CREAM

1½ TEASPOONS PURE VANILLA EXTRACT

¾ CUP BUTTERMILK

¾ POUND SOLID VEGETABLE SHORTENING PER QUART FRYER CAPACITY (FOR A 4-QUART FRYER USE 3 POUNDS SHORTENING)

POWDERED SUGAR, FOR DUSTING (OPTIONAL)

Sift together the first nine ingredients, mixing well. Mix together the sugar and potatoes. Then add the melted butter, eggs, egg yolks, and honey, and combine thoroughly. Add the sour cream and vanilla. Mix well. Add the buttermilk and stir thoroughly. Add the dry sifted ingredients to the wet mixture, stir, and chill in the refrigerator for 20 minutes, until the dough becomes a bit stiffer.

While the dough chills, slowly heat the shortening until it reaches 352°F. Monitor it carefully so it does not get too hot. These doughnuts are rolled out, cut, and fried the same way as the Dunky Oaty Doughnuts (page 27), though you would use all-purpose unbleached flour to flour the board when rolling out the dough.

MAKES ABOUT 1 DOZEN DOUGHNUTS

Whole Wheat Orange Doughnuts

This is the only recipe from another source that we were able to use as is. It comes from Gourmet magazine and the doughnuts have the distinction of being very good not only right after they are fried but for many hours afterward. They are also particularly good frozen and reheated.

3³/₄ CUPS PASTRY FLOUR

2 TEASPOONS BAKING POWDER

1 TEASPOON BAKING SODA

1 TEASPOON POWDERED GINGER

³/₄ TEASPOON GROUND NUTMEG

¹/₂ TEASPOON SALT

¹/₂ TEASPOON GROUND ALLSPICE

2 CUPS WHOLE WHEAT FLOUR (FINELY GROUND, PREFERABLY)

4 EGGS

1 CUP DARK BROWN SUGAR

¹/₂ CUP GRANULATED SUGAR

1 ¹/₂ CUPS BUTTERMILK

4 OUNCES BUTTER, MELTED (¹/₂ CUP)

1 TABLESPOON GRATED ORANGE RIND OR 1 TEASPOON ORANGE OIL

³/₄ POUND SOLID VEGETABLE SHORTENING PER QUART CAPACITY FRYER (FOR A 4-QUART FRYER, USE ABOUT 3 POUNDS SHORTENING)

Sift together the first seven ingredients, then add the whole wheat flour, combining it thoroughly. Mix together the eggs and brown and granulated sugars. Add the buttermilk, melted butter, and orange rind (or orange oil). Combine the wet and dry ingredients, but do not overmix. Chill the dough in the refrigerator, for about 20 minutes and proceed to roll out, cut, and fry, as for Dunky Oaty Doughnuts (page 27).

MAKES ABOUT 1¹/₂ DOZEN DOUGHNUTS

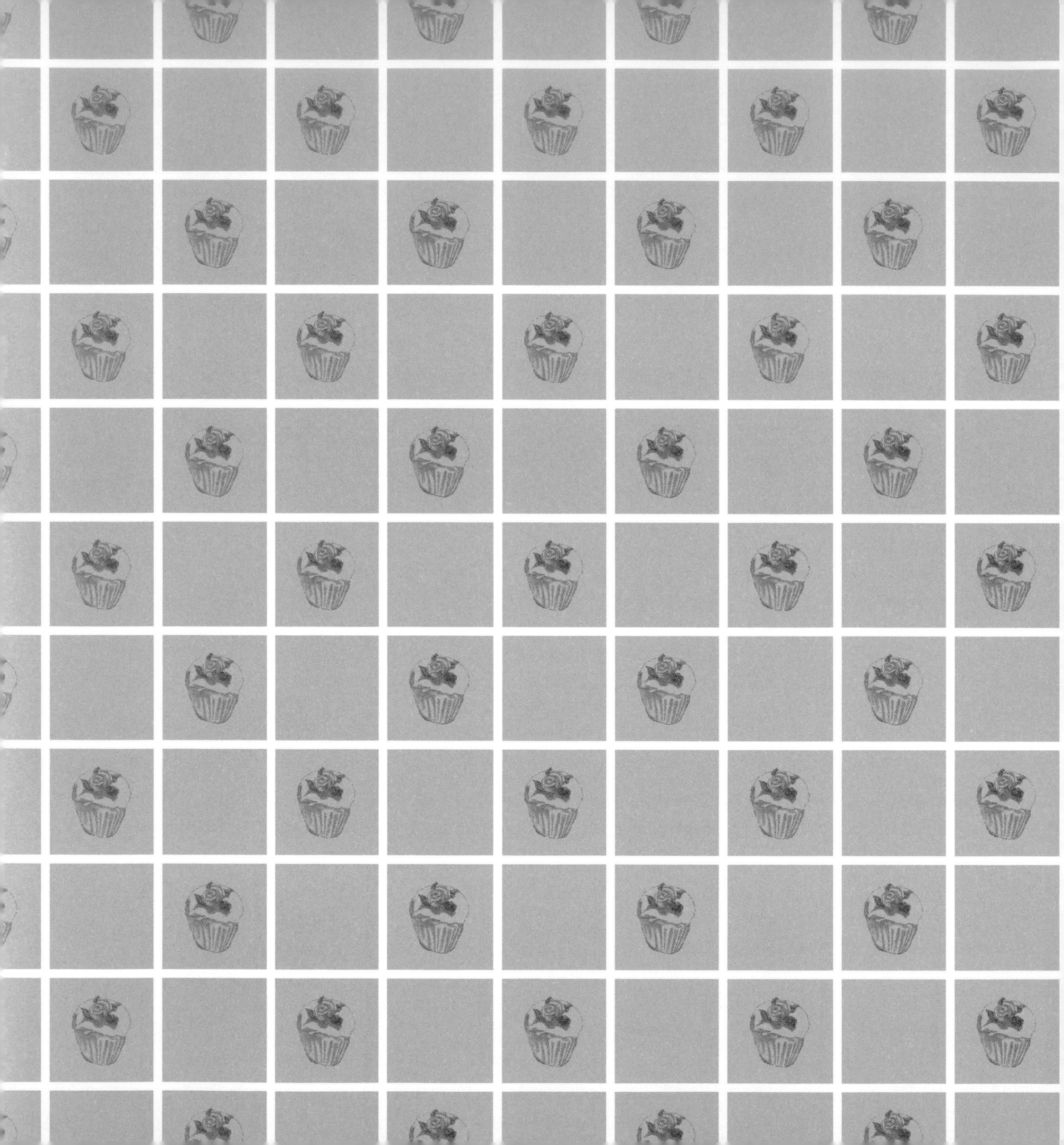

Long Island Crullers

This is another plain vanilla doughnut. It is richer and has a crustier texture than the
Buttermilk Skies (page 31).

4 CUPS SIFTED ALL-PURPOSE FLOUR

1 TABLESPOON BAKING POWDER

1 TABLESPOON GROUND NUTMEG

1 1/2 TEASPOONS SALT

2 EGGS PLUS 1 EXTRA YOLK

1 CUP SUGAR

1 TABLESPOON PURE VANILLA EXTRACT

2 OUNCES BUTTER, MELTED (1/4 CUP)

1 CUP MILK

3/4 POUND SOLID VEGETABLE
SHORTENING PER QUART FRYER
CAPACITY

CONFECTIONERS' SUGAR, FOR DUSTING

Sift together the flour, baking powder, nutmeg, and salt. Beat together the eggs, egg yolk, and sugar. Add the vanilla, melted butter, and milk. Mix the wet ingredients into the dry, and chill the dough in the refrigerator for 20 to 30 minutes to firm up and make handling easier. Roll, cut, and fry as for Dunky Oaty Doughnuts (page 27).

Dust with confectioners' sugar when cool.

MAKES ABOUT 1 1/2 DOZEN DOUGHNUTS

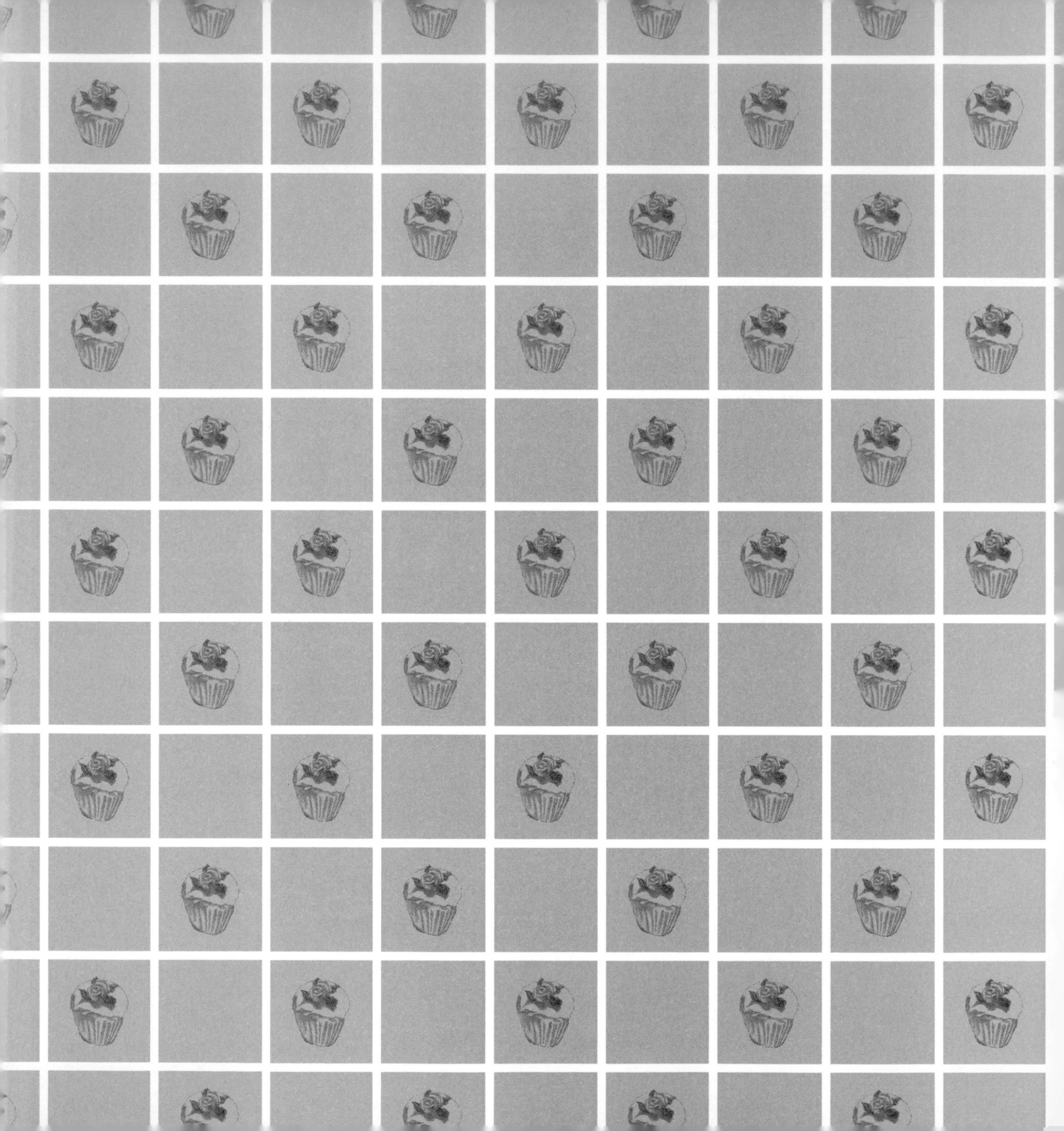

Pumpkin Doughnuts

This recipe came from a friend's mother, Joy Smith Rogers, of Waterville and Ellsworth, Maine, who got it from her Aunt Hazel. It takes an interesting sweet flavor from the pumpkin.

⅔ CUP SUGAR

1 EGG

¾ TEASPOON PURE VANILLA
EXTRACT

¾ CUP PUREED PUMPKIN (CANNED OR
FRESH-COOKED)

1 CUP BUTTERMILK

1 OUNCE BUTTER, MELTED
(2 TABLESPOONS)

3½ CUPS ALL-PURPOSE FLOUR

1 TABLESPOON BAKING POWDER

½ TEASPOON SALT

1 TEASPOON GROUND NUTMEG

1 POUND SOLID VEGETABLE
SHORTENING PER QUART FRYER
CAPACITY

Mix the sugar, egg, and vanilla together with the pumpkin. Add the buttermilk and melted butter. Sift together the flour, baking powder, salt, and nutmeg. Combine the wet and dry ingredients and chill the dough for 20 minutes or longer until it has firmed up and is easy to handle. Roll, cut, and fry as for Dunky Oaty Doughnuts (page 27).

MAKES ABOUT 1 DOZEN DOUGHNUTS

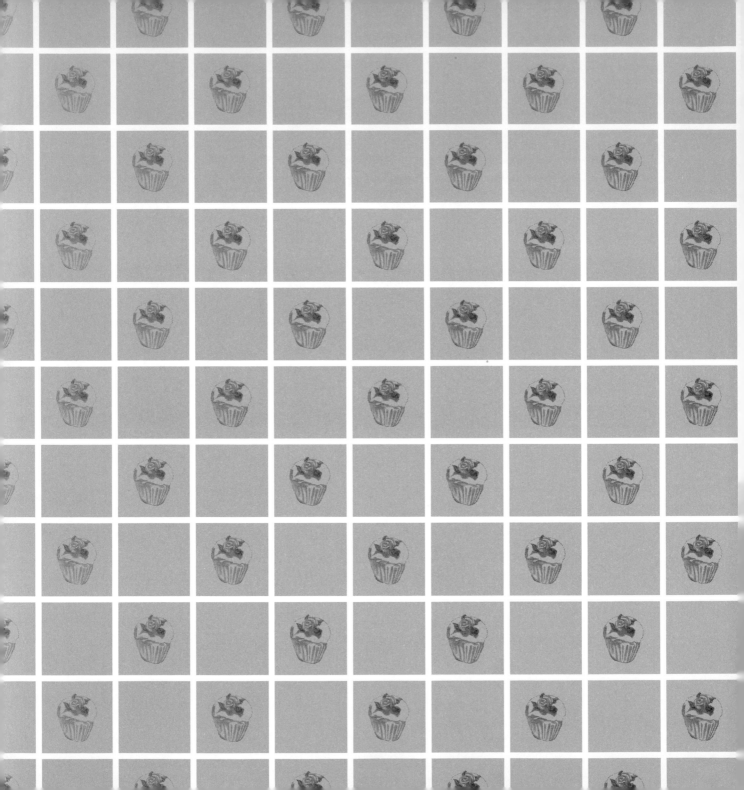

Breakfast Baked Goods

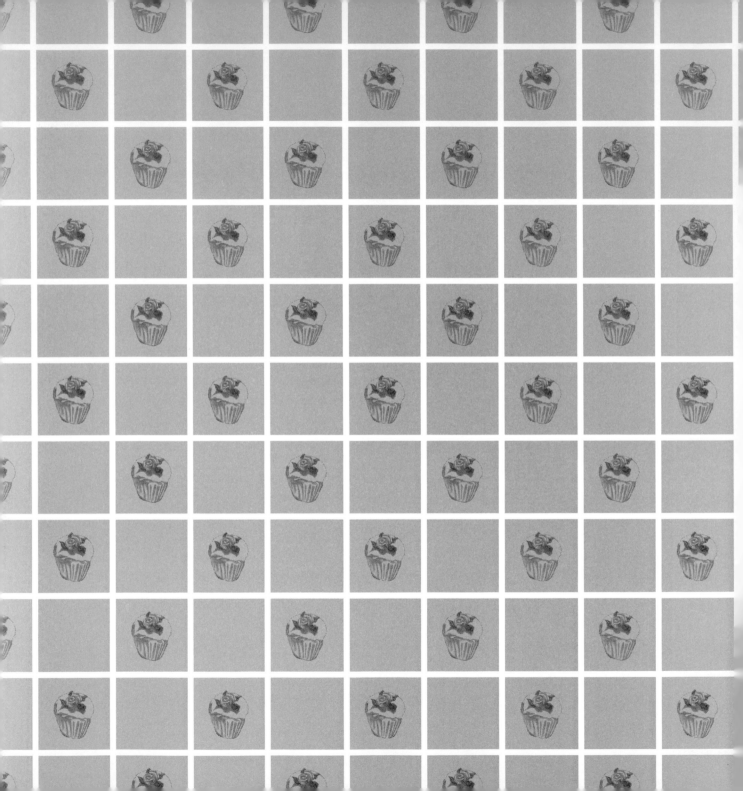

Muffins

The year the Cupcake Café opened, 1988, was the height of a still-not-quite-subsided muffin craze; anyone selling breakfast had to offer muffins. (This is when muffins started to balloon to the slow-pitch softball size still widely available today.)

While it is true that during my high school years my standard morning fare was a corn muffin (if I'm ever the subject of a Senate confirmation hearing, someone will probably come forward and report that I once dropped crumbs in their hair while they sat on an uptown Lexington Avenue subway), as an adult, my interest in muffins had been minimal. Until we were commercially motivated to pay attention to the muffin, my only interest lay in the remote possibility of ever finding enough blueberries in a blueberry muffin to make it worth eating, and a perverse and personal desire to find a bran muffin less sweet than a cupcake.

Forced to turn our attention to muffins, we tried to come up with muffins reminiscent of the quick bread we grew up with, and less like commercial snack cakes. These recipes use less oil (and more butter) and less sugar than typical commercial muffins. The result is a muffin that is neither greasy nor too sweet. And the bran and oat bran are certifiably good for you.

Most people complain (when they're not complaining about something else) that there isn't enough fruit in fruit muffins, so the Cupcake Café took the innovative step of including more fruit! (And we didn't pay a marketing consultant for that advice.) This does mean that in some cases, the blueberry being one, the fruit may sink to the bottom. But they still taste good, and no one has complained about a lack of fruit in our muffins.

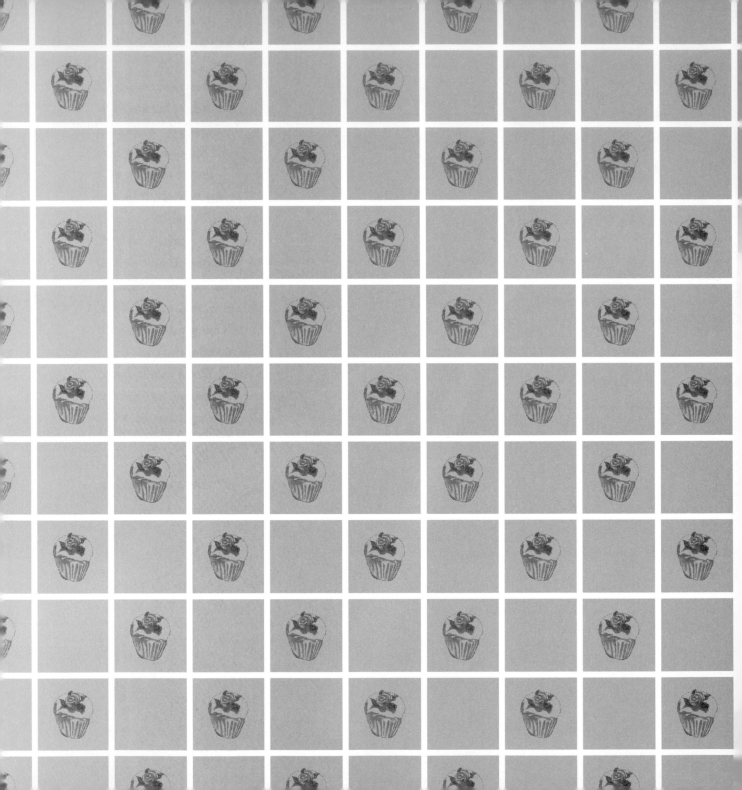

Irish Soda Muffins

3 CUPS ALL-PURPOSE FLOUR

1/2 TEASPOON SALT

1 1/2 TEASPOONS BAKING SODA

1 1/2 TABLESPOONS CARAWAY SEEDS

1/2 CUP DARK SEEDLESS RAISINS

4 OUNCES BUTTER, MELTED (1/2 CUP)

1/2 CUP HONEY

2 EGGS

1 1/2 CUPS BUTTERMILK

2 TEASPOONS LEMON JUICE

Grease an 8-cup muffin tin. Preheat the oven to 350°F. Sift together the flour, salt, and baking soda. Add the caraway seeds and raisins. Mix together the melted butter, honey, and eggs, then add the buttermilk and lemon juice. Lightly combine the dry and wet ingredients but do not overmix!

Spoon the batter into the cups of the greased muffin tin and bake for about 20 to 25 minutes, until a straw or cake tester inserted in the center comes out clean or the muffin feels springy when pressed gently with your finger.

MAKES 8 MUFFINS

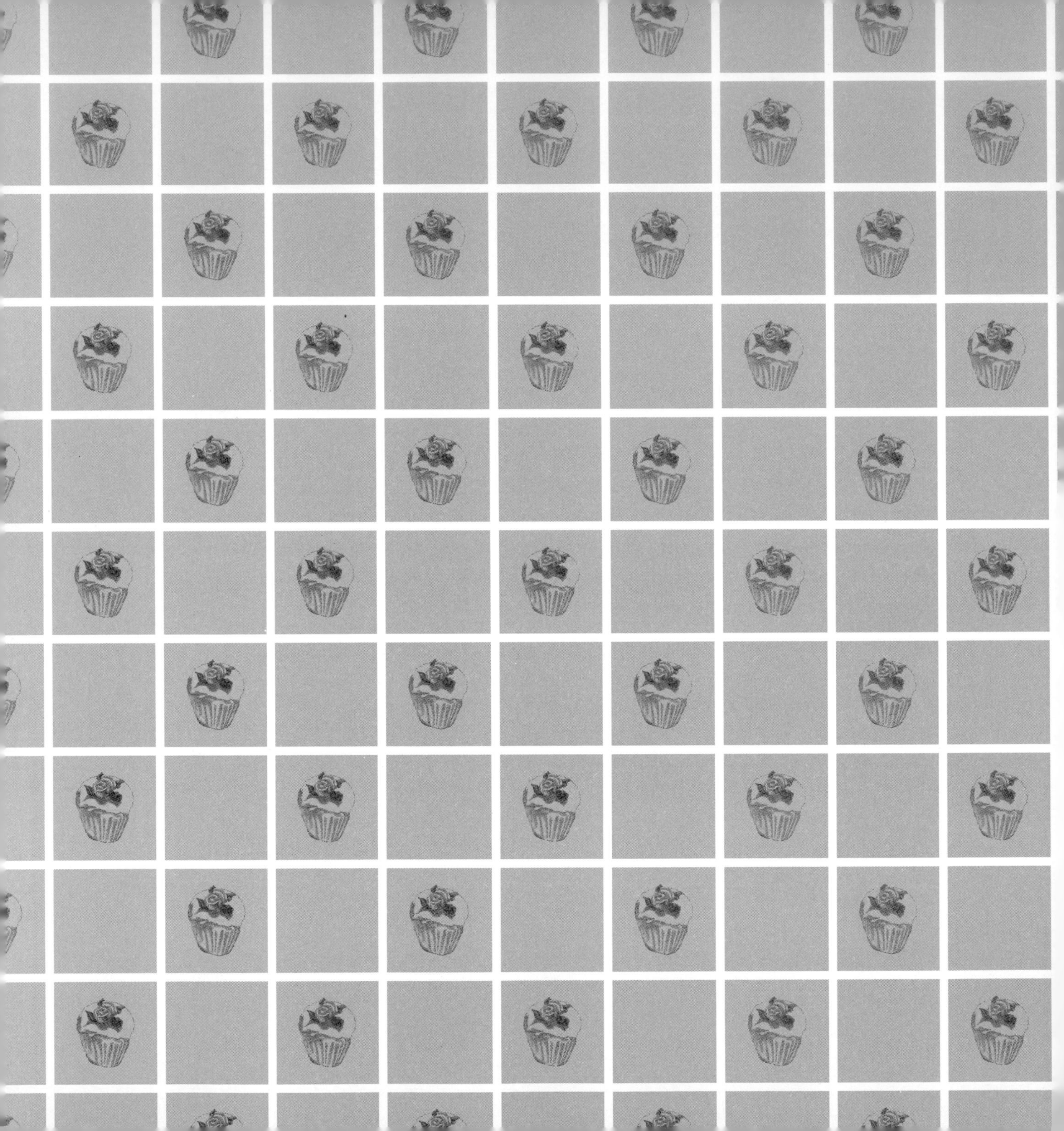

Lemon Poppy Seed Muffins

½ POUND SWEET BUTTER (1 CUP)

1 ⅓ CUPS SUGAR

4 EGGS

2 TEASPOONS GRATED LEMON RIND OR
  ½ TEASPOON LEMON OIL

1 TEASPOON PURE VANILLA EXTRACT

2 ⅔ CUPS UNBLEACHED FLOUR

½ TEASPOON BAKING POWDER

1 TEASPOON BAKING SODA

½ TEASPOON SALT

½ CUP POPPY SEEDS

1 CUP BUTTERMILK

Grease a 12-cup muffin tin. Preheat the oven to 350°F. Cream together the butter and sugar. Add the eggs, lemon rind (or oil), and vanilla. Sift together the flour, baking powder, baking soda, and salt. Mix in the poppy seeds, distributing them evenly throughout the flour mix. Add the flour mix to the butter mixture along with the buttermilk, until just combined. Bake in the greased muffin cups for about 25 to 30 minutes, until a straw or cake tester inserted in the center comes out clean or the muffin feels springy when pressed gently with your finger.

MAKES 1 DOZEN MUFFINS

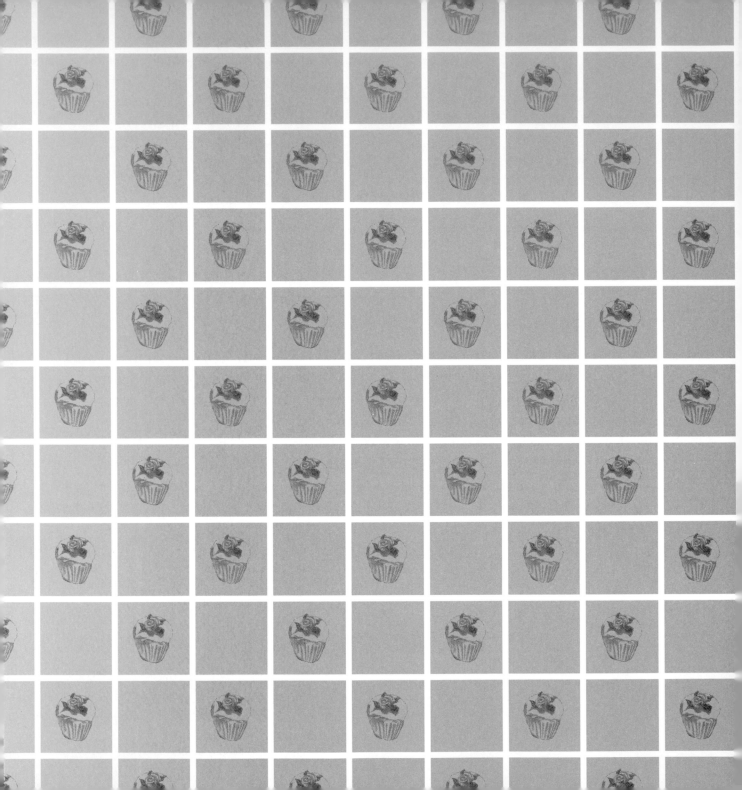

Cranberry Muffins

3 1/4 CUPS UNBLEACHED FLOUR

3/4 CUP WHOLE WHEAT FLOUR

2 1/2 TEASPOONS BAKING POWDER

1 TEASPOON BAKING SODA

1/2 TEASPOON SALT

1 1/2 CUPS SUGAR

2 OUNCES BUTTER (1/4 CUP)

3 EGGS

1 1/2 CUPS ORANGE JUICE

1 TABLESPOON GRATED ORANGE RIND

2 1/2 CUPS COARSELY CHOPPED
   CRANBERRIES*

1 CUP CHOPPED WALNUTS

Butter a 12-cup muffin tin or line the cups with muffin papers. Preheat the oven to 350°F. Combine the flours, baking powder, baking soda and salt. Cream together the sugar with the butter, then beat in the eggs. Add the orange juice and orange rind to the eggs. Toss the chopped cranberries and walnuts into the flour mix, distributing them well throughout. Add the egg and orange juice mixture to the flour mixture and mix until just combined. Fill the muffin cups two-thirds full and bake about 35 to 40 minutes until a straw or cake tester inserted in the center comes out clean or the muffin feels springy when pressed gently with your finger.

MAKES 1 DOZEN MUFFINS

*Chop cranberries with a food processor if you have one, but don't overdo it, a few quick pulses should do. Or use a knife, just halving or quartering the cranberries.

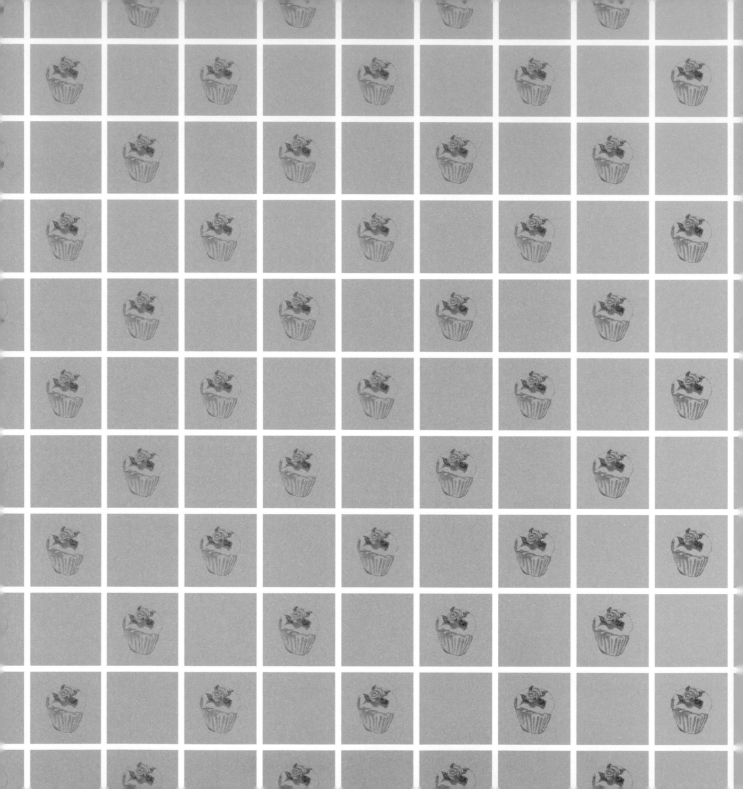

Apple Muffins

3 TO 3 1/2 CUPS PEELED AND CUBED
APPLES SUCH AS GOLDEN
DELICIOUS, MCINTOSH, GALA,
NORTHERN SPY, OR GRANNY SMITH
(2 TO 3 POUNDS APPLES)

1 TEASPOON LEMON JUICE

1/2 CUP PLUS 1 TABLESPOON HONEY

2/3 CUP VEGETABLE OIL

2 EGGS BEATEN

1 TEASPOON PURE VANILLA EXTRACT

1 1/2 CUPS UNBLEACHED FLOUR

1 TEASPOON BAKING SODA

1/2 TEASPOON BAKING POWDER

1 1/2 TEASPOONS GROUND CINNAMON

1/2 TEASPOON GROUND ALLSPICE

1/2 TEASPOON SALT

1/2 CUP WHOLE WHEAT FLOUR

3/4 CUP WALNUTS

3/4 CUP DARK SEEDLESS RAISINS

Grease a 12-cup muffin tin, or line the cups with muffin papers. Preheat the oven to 350°F.

Toss the cubed apples with the lemon juice and 1/2 cup honey. Add the vegetable oil, the eggs, and the vanilla. Sift together the unbleached flour, baking soda, baking powder, cinnamon, allspice, and salt. Add the whole wheat flour, walnuts, and raisins to the dry mix and mix well. Fill the muffin cups two-thirds full and bake for about 30 minutes, until a straw or cake tester inserted in the center comes out clean or the muffin feels springy when pressed gently with your finger.

MAKES 1 DOZEN MUFFINS

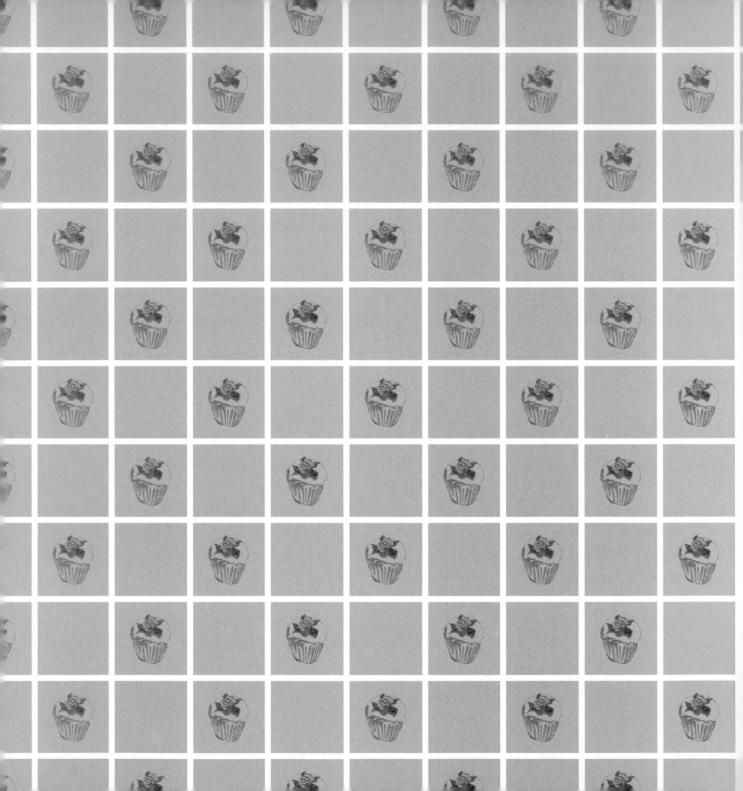

Blueberry Muffins

2 CUPS UNBLEACHED FLOUR

1 TEASPOON BAKING POWDER

1/2 TEASPOON BAKING SODA

1/2 TEASPOON SALT

1/3 CUP LIGHT BROWN SUGAR

1/4 CUP GRANULATED SUGAR

2 EGGS

1/2 CUP SOUR CREAM

2 TABLESPOONS BUTTER, MELTED
   (1 OUNCE)

1/2 CUP BUTTERMILK

1 PINT BLUEBERRIES, WASHED AND
   PICKED OVER TO ELIMINATE ANY
   QUESTIONABLE ONES

Grease 12 large or 18 smaller muffin cups, or line the cups with muffin papers. Preheat the oven to 400°F. Sift together the flour, baking powder, baking soda, and salt. Combine the sugars, eggs, sour cream, butter, and buttermilk. Toss the blueberries with the flour mixture. Add the wet mixture into the dry mixture and stir until just combined. Fill the muffin cups two-thirds full, and bake for about 25 minutes, until a cake tester or straw inserted in the center comes out clean or the muffin feels springy when pressed gently with your finger.

MAKES 12 TO 18 MUFFINS, DEPENDING ON SIZE

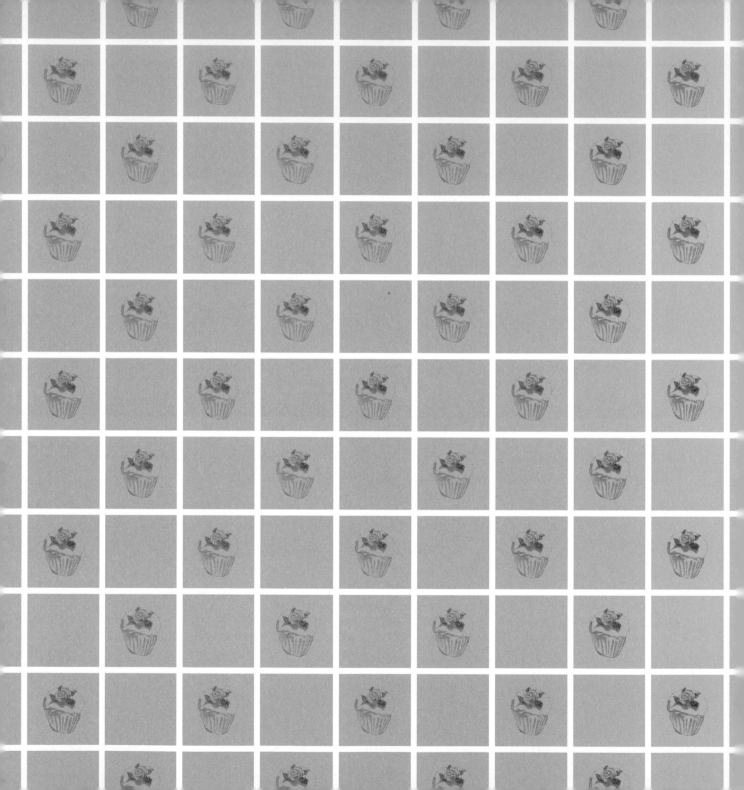

Oat Bran Muffins

½ CUP BOILING WATER

1 CUP OAT BRAN

½ CUP NONFAT DRY MILK

1 CUP OAT FLOUR (USE A FOOD
PROCESSOR TO FINELY GRIND ROLLED
OATS TO MAKE OAT FLOUR, OR
PURCHASE IT AT A HEALTH FOOD
STORE)

1 TEASPOON BAKING POWDER

1 TEASPOON BAKING SODA

½ TEASPOON SALT

½ TEASPOON GROUND CINNAMON

½ TEASPOON GROUND MACE

1 CUP OATMEAL (UNCOOKED ROLLED
OATS)

½ CUP DARK SEEDLESS RAISINS

2 TABLESPOONS MOLASSES

1 ¼ CUPS BUTTERMILK

¼ CUP VEGETABLE OIL

1 LARGE APPLE, CORED, PEELED, AND
FINELY DICED

1 TEASPOON GRATED ORANGE RIND

6 EGG WHITES

Grease an 8-cup muffin tin or line the cups with muffin papers. Preheat the oven to 350°F. Pour the boiling water over the oat bran. Set aside. Mix together the dry milk, oat flour, baking powder, baking soda, salt, cinnamon, mace, oatmeal, and raisins. Mix together molasses, buttermilk, oil, apple, and orange rind into the water and oat bran. Beat the egg whites until they are just slightly stiff.

Mix together the wet and dry ingredients until just combined, then fold in the beaten egg whites. Bake in the muffin cups for 25 to 30 minutes, until a straw or cake tester comes out clean or the muffin feels springy when pressed gently with your finger.

MAKES 8 MUFFINS

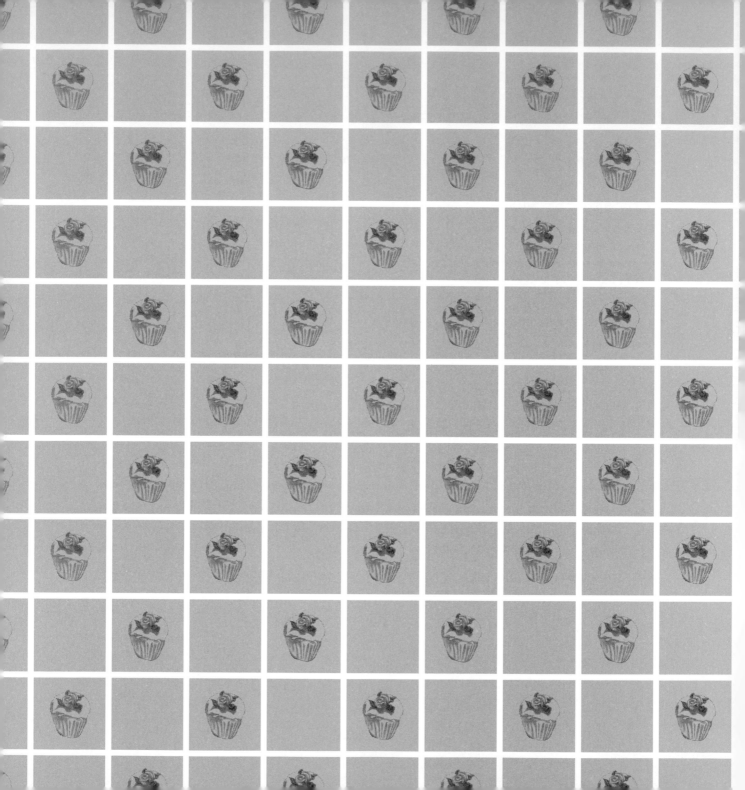

Banana Muffins

2 1/2 CUPS UNBLEACHED FLOUR

2 TEASPOONS BAKING POWDER

1 TEASPOON BAKING SODA

1/2 TEASPOON SALT

2/3 CUP CHOPPED WALNUTS

1/4 POUND BUTTER (4 OUNCES)

3/4 CUP SUGAR

3 EGGS

1 1/2 CUPS THOROUGHLY MASHED OR
PUREED VERY RIPE BANANAS

Grease 8 large or 12 smaller muffin cups, or line them with muffin papers. Preheat the oven to 350°F. Sift together the flour, baking powder, baking soda, and salt. Add the walnuts. Cream together the butter and sugar. Beat in the eggs one at a time. Mix the banana into the egg mixture. Fold in the dry ingredients until just blended. Fill the cups two-thirds full and bake for 25 to 35 minutes, depending on the size of your muffin tins. They are done when a straw or cake tester inserted in the center comes out clean or the muffin feels springy when pressed gently with your finger.

MAKES 8 LARGE OR 12 SMALL MUFFINS

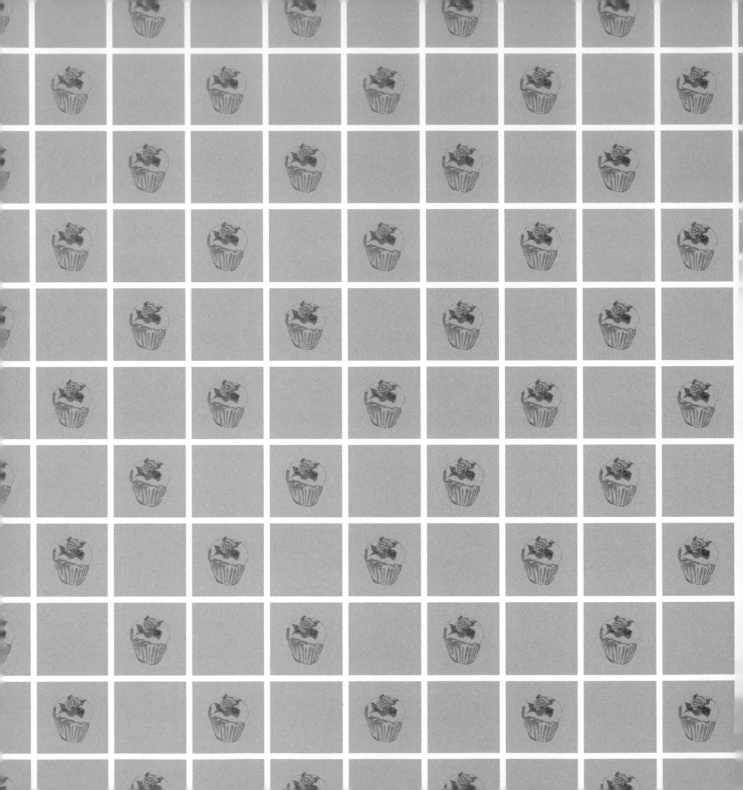

Bran Muffins

1 CUP BRAN

1 CUP BOILING WATER

4 OUNCES BUTTER (¼ POUND)

¼ CUP HONEY

1 ½ CUPS WHOLE WHEAT FLOUR

1 ½ TEASPOONS BAKING SODA

⅓ CUP DRY POWDERED MILK

½ TEASPOON SALT

½ CUP WHEAT GERM

2 EGGS

1 CUP BUTTERMILK

1 CUP DARK SEEDLESS RAISINS

Grease an 8-cup muffin tin or line the cups with muffin papers. Preheat the oven to 350°F. Combine the bran, boiling water, butter, and honey. Mix together well with the whole wheat flour, baking soda, powdered milk, salt, and wheat germ.

Mix the eggs and buttermilk together. Add the bran mixture. Add the raisins and the dry mix. Stir together until just combined. Bake in the muffin cups for about 25 minutes. The muffins are done when a straw or cake tester inserted in the center comes out clean and the muffin feels springy when pressed gently with your finger.

MAKES 8 MUFFINS

Zucchini Muffins

1 ³/₄ CUPS ALL-PURPOSE FLOUR

¹/₂ TEASPOON SALT

³/₄ TEASPOON BAKING SODA

¹/₂ TEASPOON BAKING POWDER

1 ¹/₂ TEASPOONS GROUND CINNAMON

¹/₂ TEASPOON GROUND GINGER

¹/₂ TEASPOON GROUND NUTMEG

²/₃ CUP GRANULATED SUGAR

¹/₃ CUP DARK BROWN SUGAR

2 EGGS

¹/₂ CUP VEGETABLE OIL

1 ¹/₂ TEASPOONS PURE VANILLA
    EXTRACT

1 TEASPOON GRATED LEMON RIND

2 CUPS GRATED ZUCCHINI*

Grease 12 large or 18 smaller muffin cups, or line the cups with muffin papers. Preheat the oven to 350°F. Sift the flour, salt, baking soda, baking powder, and spices together. Mix together the brown and white sugars and the eggs; add to this the vegetable oil, vanilla, and lemon rind. Stir in the grated zucchini. Add the flour mixture, combining everything but not overmixing. Fill the muffin cups two-thirds full and bake about 25 minutes, until a straw or cake tester inserted in the center comes out clean or the muffin feels springy when pressed gently with your finger.

MAKES 12 TO 18 MUFFINS, DEPENDING ON SIZE

*Use as much green rind as you can. A hand grater works best; the results from a food processor tend to be too wet.

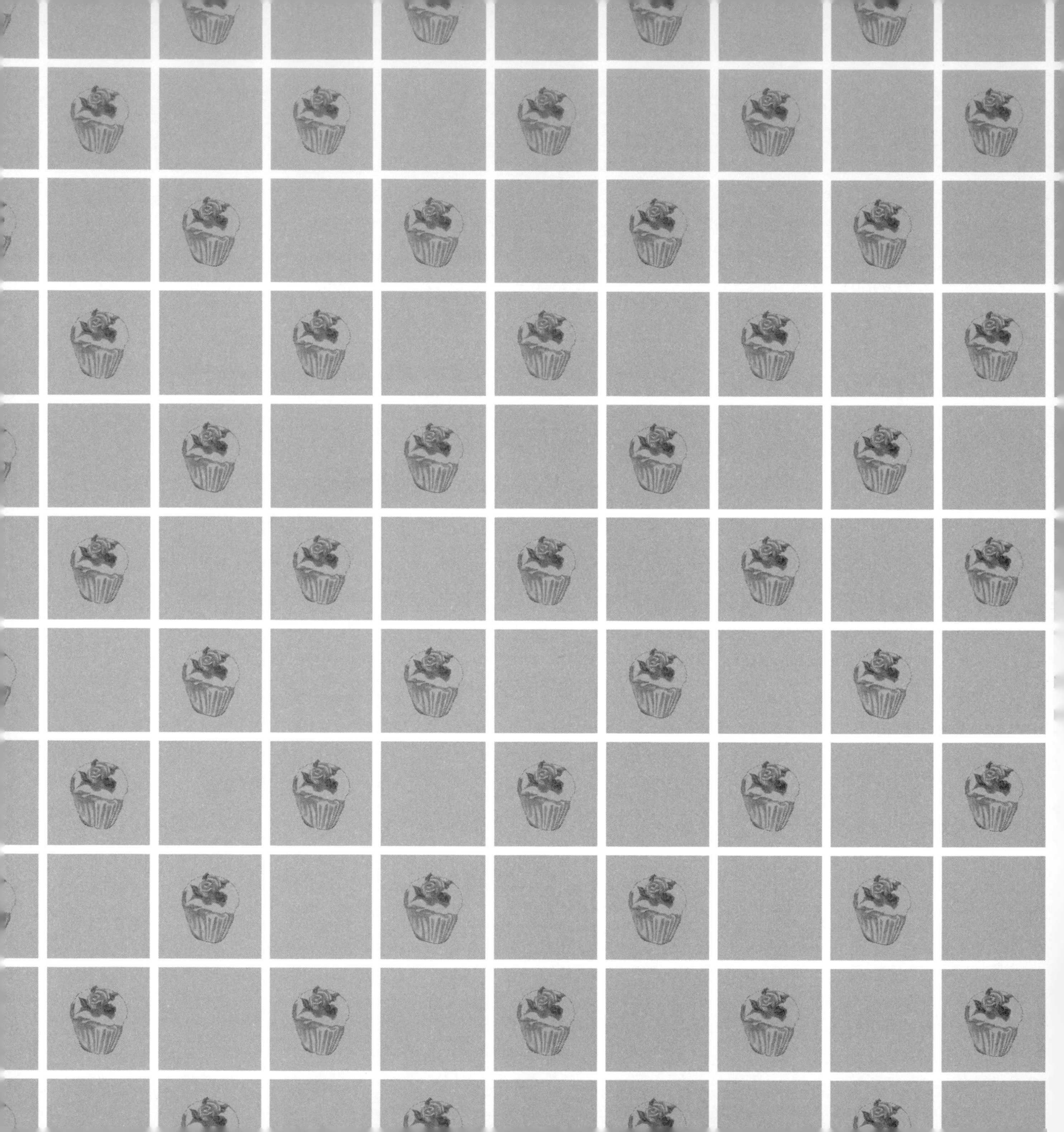

Corn Muffins

1 CUP PASTRY FLOUR	¼ CUP DRY POWDERED MILK
1 CUP UNBLEACHED FLOUR	¾ CUP SUGAR
1 TABLESPOON BAKING POWDER	3 EGGS
½ TEASPOON SALT	8 OUNCES BUTTER, MELTED (½ CUP)
1 ½ CUPS CORNMEAL	2 CUPS COLD WATER

Grease 12 large or 18 smaller muffin cups or line them with muffin papers. Preheat the oven to 350°F.

Sift together the pastry flour, unbleached flour, baking powder, and salt. Add the cornmeal and powdered milk and mix well. Stir in the sugar. Mix well. Beat the eggs, then add the melted butter and water. Stir the egg mixture into the flour and cornmeal mixture until just combined. Do not overmix.

Bake in the greased or lined muffin cups for 25 to 35 minutes, until a straw or cake tester inserted in the center comes out clean or the muffin feels springy when pressed gently with your finger.

MAKES 12 TO 18 MUFFINS

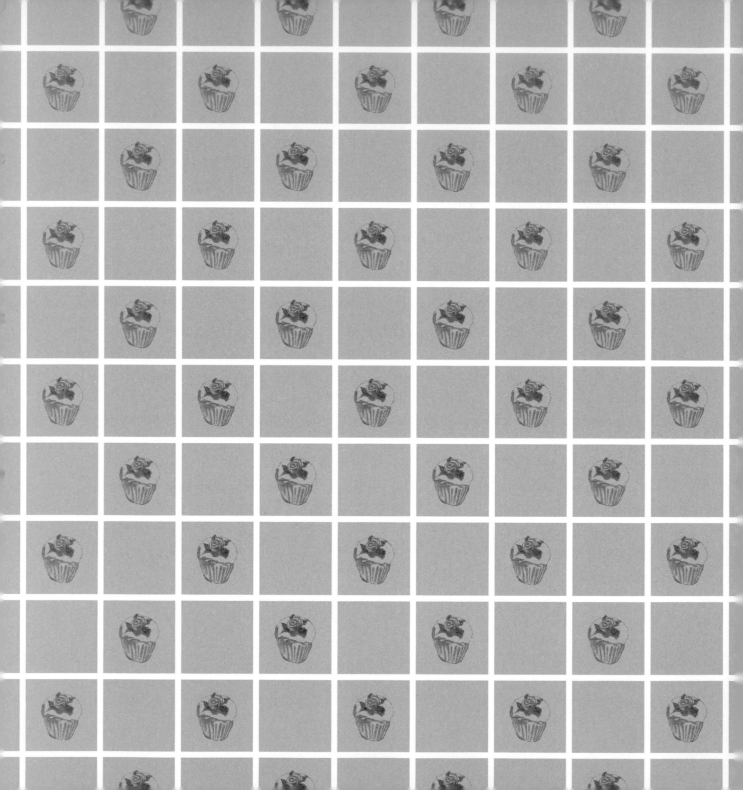

Pecan Harvest Loaf

1 ½ CUPS ALL-PURPOSE FLOUR

1 TEASPOON BAKING POWDER

¼ TEASPOON SALT

1 ⅓ CUPS TOASTED PECANS, COARSELY
  GROUND

5 OUNCES BUTTER

½ CUP GRANULATED SUGAR

½ CUP DARK BROWN SUGAR

4 EGGS, SEPARATED

3 TABLESPOONS MILK

1 TABLESPOON PLUS 1 TEASPOON
  STRONG BREWED COFFEE

½ TEASPOON PURE VANILLA EXTRACT

1 RECIPE LEMON GLAZE
  (RECIPE FOLLOWS)

Grease an 8 × 4-inch loaf pan and preheat the oven to 350°F. Sift the flour with the baking powder and salt. Add the ground pecans and mix well. Cream the butter and sugars and add the egg yolks, milk, coffee, and vanilla. Beat the egg whites till stiff but not dry. Add the flour and pecans to the wet ingredients. When just combined, fold in the egg whites.

Pour the batter into the prepared pan and bake for 45 to 50 minutes, until done. (Insert a straw or cake tester into the center of the loaf. If it comes out clean, it's done, or if loaf has a springy feel when you press on it.) Allow to cool slightly, then glaze with Lemon Glaze.

YIELD: 1 LOAF

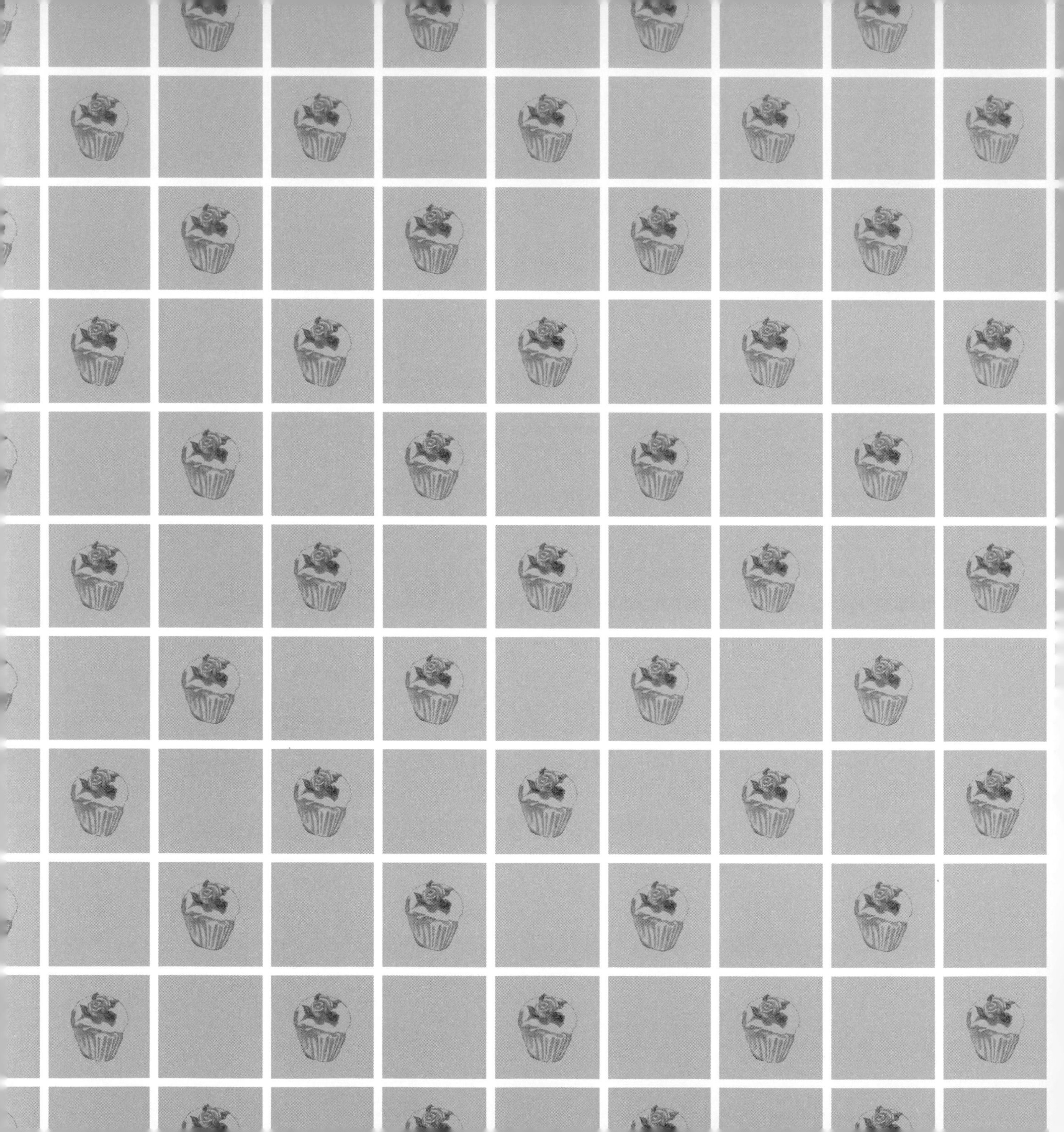

Lemon Glaze

¹/₄ CUP FRESH LEMON JUICE   1 ¹/₂ CUPS SUGAR

Combine the lemon juice and sugar in a small saucepan and cook over medium heat, stirring, for 10 to 15 minutes, until transparent. Test to see if the syrup forms a "string" when dropped from a spoon. When it does, take it off the heat and spoon it over the slightly cooled pecan harvest loaf.

MAKES 1³/₄ CUPS GLAZE, ENOUGH FOR 1 PECAN HARVEST LOAF

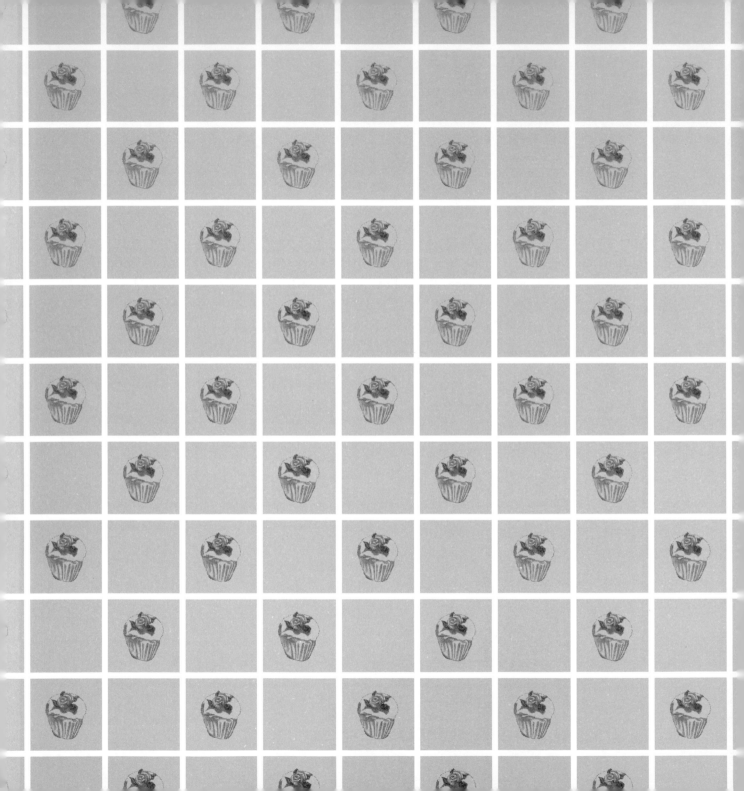

Waffles

*The Cupcake doesn't make French toast or pancakes, or anything else on a grill, just waffles.
The reason for this is that we happened to have a collection of old waffle irons on hand when we opened
the Café. (So far no culinary outlet has been found for Michael's collection of old typewriters.)
This waffle recipe was handed down to me by my Aunt Hadi, who got it from her father, who was famous
in some limited circles for his waffles. The now-divulged family secret is to beat the egg whites
separately before adding them to the rest of the mixture.*

4 CUPS ALL-PURPOSE FLOUR

1 TABLESPOON PLUS 1 TEASPOON
BAKING POWDER

1 TEASPOON SALT

1 TABLESPOON SUGAR

6 EGGS, CAREFULLY SEPARATED

½ POUND BUTTER, MELTED

1 ½ CUPS WHOLE MILK

1 ¾ CUPS BUTTERMILK

Sift together the flour, baking powder, and salt. Add the sugar. Beat the 6 egg yolks. Add the melted butter, milk, and buttermilk to the yolks. Beat the egg whites until stiff but not dry. Add the milk mixture to the dry ingredients, just until combined. Fold in the egg whites.

Preheat a waffle iron and grease it with butter before making the first waffle. Pour on just enough batter to cover the center of the iron surface—don't overfill it. Waffle irons vary, so follow the manufacturer's instructions. (Some waffle irons, for instance, light when the waffle is done; others come with a built-in timer.) Generally speaking, waffles take about 4 to 5 minutes, until nicely brown and easy to remove from the iron.

MAKES ABOUT 6 TO 8 WAFFLES

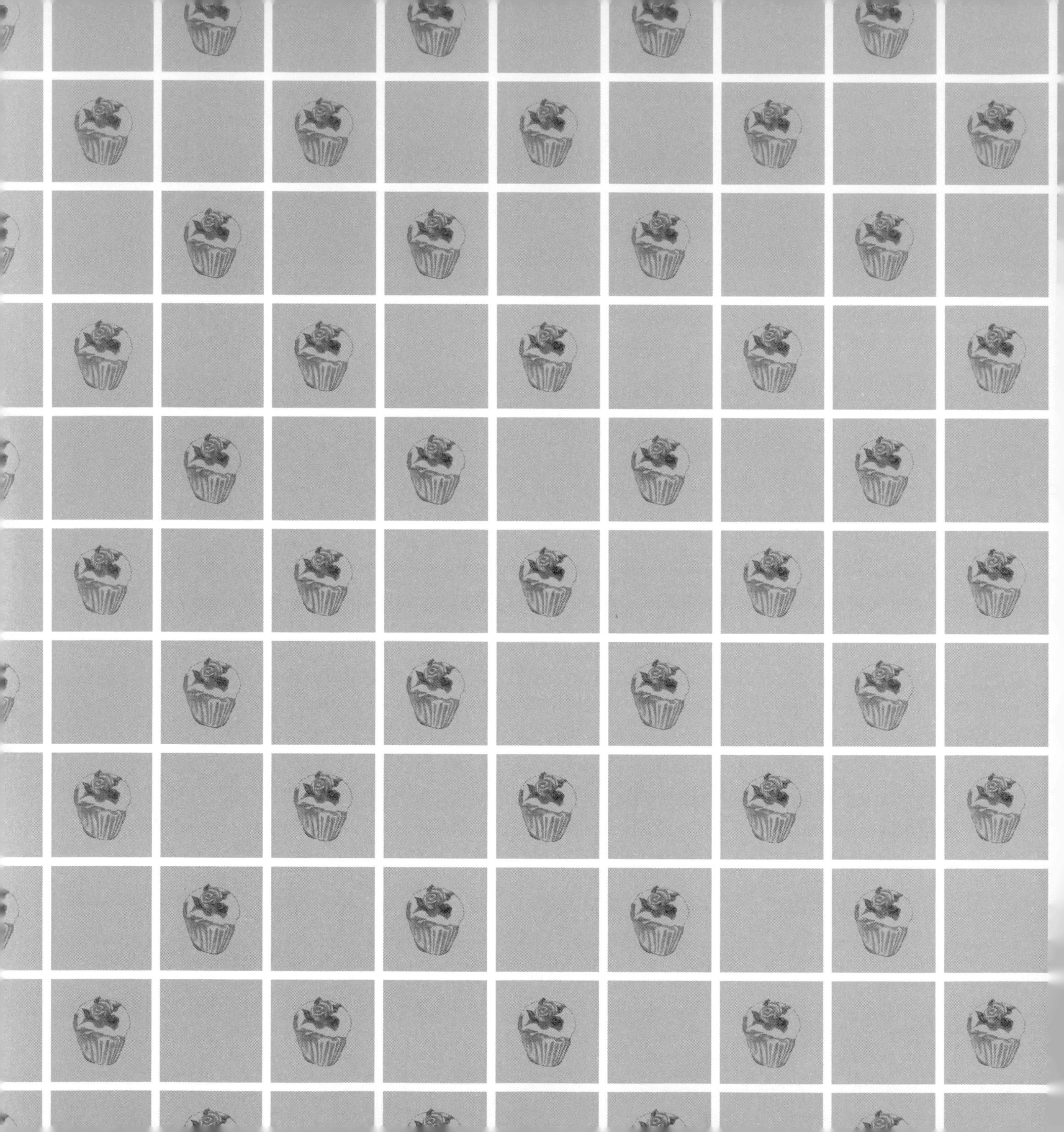

Raisin Scones

This recipe comes from Cupcake veteran Nora Byron's mother, who lives in County Tipperary (where they call these "fruit scones"). When she learned that her daughter had imported her scones to New York, she declared, "Well, they're not getting my Irish soda bread." Special care should be taken when making these scones not to overwork the flour and butter, which will cause the butter to melt prematurely and ultimately produce a tough product.

4 CUPS ALL-PURPOSE FLOUR

½ TEASPOON BAKING POWDER

4 OUNCES COLD BUTTER, CUT UP
(8 TABLESPOONS)

¼ CUP SUGAR

1 CUP DARK SEEDLESS RAISINS

1 EGG

1 CUP MILK

Egg wash
½ CUP MILK AND 1 EGG MIXED
TOGETHER

Preheat the oven to 400°F. Grease and flour a baking sheet. Sift the flour and baking powder together into a bowl. Rub in the butter quickly and lightly until the flour and butter are flaky. Add the sugar and raisins and mix lightly. Beat the egg and milk together with a whisk, add to the flour mixture, and knead lightly to form a soft dough. Do not overknead; add a little more milk if necessary to keep dough from becoming too floury or tough. With floured hands, roll with a rolling pin the dough out evenly to 1½-inch thickness. Cut out scones with a circular pastry cutter (a 2-inch diameter works) using a quick sharp motion—do not twist the cutter or the scones will distort as they bake.

Brush with the egg wash mixture. Bake on the prepared baking sheet for 10 minutes at 400°F. Then reduce the heat to 300°F and continue to bake for an additional 20 minutes, or until the scones have a nice golden brown glow.

MAKES ABOUT 10 SCONES

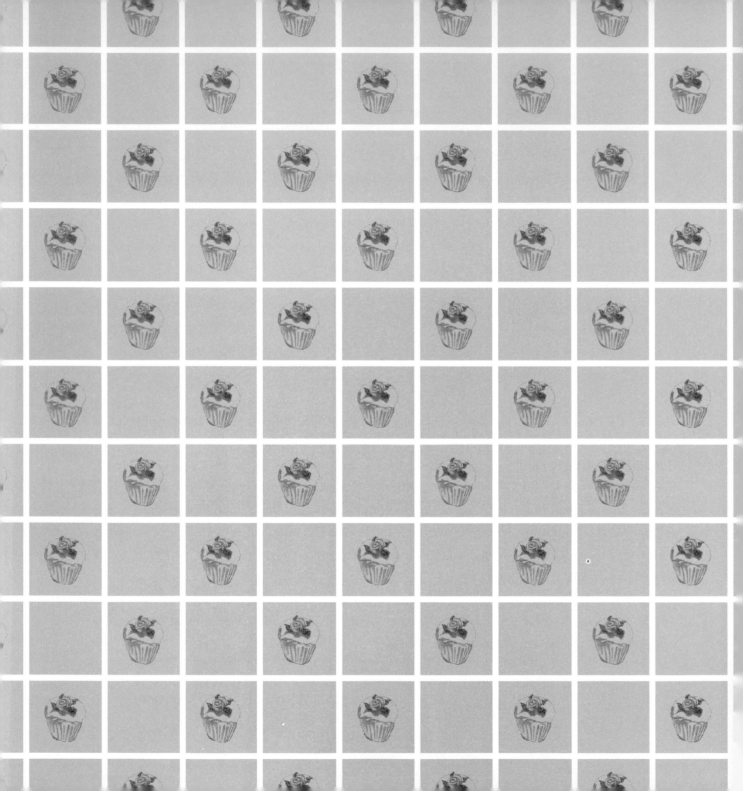

Plain Coffee Cake

This sour cream coffee cake is especially popular among very early risers. It provides a good base for that first cup of coffee.

Batter

3 CUPS ALL-PURPOSE FLOUR

1 TABLESPOON BAKING POWDER

1 TEASPOON BAKING SODA

1/2 TEASPOON SALT

1 1/2 CUPS GRANULATED SUGAR

4 EGGS

2 CUPS SOUR CREAM

Streusel Topping

1/3 CUP FLOUR

2/3 CUP DARK BROWN SUGAR

1 1/2 TEASPOONS GROUND CINNAMON

2 TO 3 TABLESPOONS COLD BUTTER, CUT UP

Thoroughly grease a 10-inch round cake pan or a 9 × 12-inch pan. Preheat the oven to 350°F.

For the coffee cake, sift the flour, baking powder, baking soda, and salt together. Add the sugar and mix thoroughly. Beat the eggs and add the sour cream, combining very well. Add the flour to the eggs and sour cream, stirring until just combined. For the streusel, mix the flour, brown sugar, and cinnamon together and rub in the butter with your fingers, or use a spoon or fork.

Pour the batter into the prepared cake pan. Cover with the streusel and bake for about 40 to 45 minutes. Insert a straw or cake tester into the center of the coffee cake; if it comes out clean (i.e., without any batter sticking to it), the coffee cake is done.

MAKES ONE 9 × 12-INCH CAKE OR ONE 10-INCH ROUND CAKE

APPLE COFFEE CAKE

Core, peel, and slice 2 or 3 Granny Smith or Golden Delicious apples. Cover the top of the coffee cake with the apple slices, then cover with the streusel topping and bake at 350°F for about 40 to 45 minutes, or until the apples feel tender when pierced with a fork.

BLUEBERRY COFFEE CAKE

Blueberries may be used in the same manner as in the apple coffee cake to make Blueberry Coffee Cake. Distribute over the coffee cake and cover with the streusel topping. Use about 1 pint, washed, stems removed, and picked over. Bake at 350°F for about 35 minutes.

PEACH COFFEE CAKE

Peel and slice about 4 fresh peaches. Lay the slices over the coffee cake batter and sprinkle the streusel topping over the sliced peaches. Bake at 350°F for about 35 to 40 minutes.

Sticky Buns

2 OUNCES FRESH CAKE YEAST

½ CUP TEPID WATER (95° TO 100°F),
    PLUS 1 CUP WATER

½ CUP PLUS 1 TABLESPOON SUGAR

6 TABLESPOONS BUTTER (3 OUNCES),
    PLUS 4 TABLESPOONS BUTTER,
    SOFTENED (2 OUNCES)

⅔ CUP COOKED AND RICED POTATO
    (ABOUT 2 TO 3 POTATOES,
    DEPENDING ON SIZE)

2 EGGS

2 TEASPOONS GRATED LEMON RIND

1 TEASPOON SALT

4 CUPS ALL-PURPOSE FLOUR

½ CUP DARK BROWN SUGAR

1 TEASPOON GROUND CINNAMON

⅔ CUP DARK SEEDLESS RAISINS

1 CUP WHOLE PECANS

Drizzle

1 CUP DARK BROWN SUGAR

⅓ CUP WATER

1 TEASPOON GRATED LEMON RIND

1 CUP KARO SYRUP

Combine the yeast with the tepid water and 1 tablespoon of the sugar and allow it to stand for 5 minutes. Check to be sure the yeast foams (i.e., "proves" it is still alive) before adding it to the rest of the ingredients. Cream together the remaining ½ cup sugar and the 6 tablespoons butter. Add the riced potato, eggs, lemon rind, and salt. Add the proofed yeast mix and 1 cup of water. Add flour just until the dough pulls away from the bowl. Add more flour if necessary. Cover with a cloth and let rise for about 45 minutes to 1 hour until doubled in bulk. The length of time it will take for a yeast dough to rise depends in part on the surrounding temperature. Times are given for "room temperature" assuming a normal room temperature. (So if it's midsummer and you don't have an air conditioner, take that into account.) Dough will rise faster in a warmer spot, but a short rising time is not always desirable for flavor, or even necessarily convenient. Even in a relatively cold spot, such as a refrigerator, yeast dough will rise, albeit quite slowly. This "retarding" of the dough can allow you to prepare sticky buns the night before and bake them in the morning. A longer rise will impart a nice yeast flavor. In a refrigerator a doubling in bulk should take about five to eight hours—longer for the first rising, shorter for a second. Wherever your dough is rising, do not try to speed things along by allowing your dough to get too warm. Too much heat can kill the yeast and even prematurely cook part of your dough. Roll out on a floured surface to a rectangle about 10 × 18 inches. Rub the dough with the combined brown sugar, softened butter, and cinnamon. Sprinkle on the raisins and ½ cup of the pecans. Combine the drizzle ingredients in a saucepan and heat over medium heat just until the brown sugar is melted. Dribble about one third of the drizzle over the dough and roll the whole thing up like a jelly roll.

Thoroughly butter a 12-inch round cake pan. Preheat the oven to 350°F. Slice the roll into equal pieces about 2 inches thick. Pour the remaining drizzle into the prepared pan and distribute the remaining pecans in the bottom. Arrange the sticky buns in the pan and allow them to rise again (about 40 minutes) to doubled in bulk. Bake for 35–40 minutes until browned.

MAKES 6 TO 9 BUNS

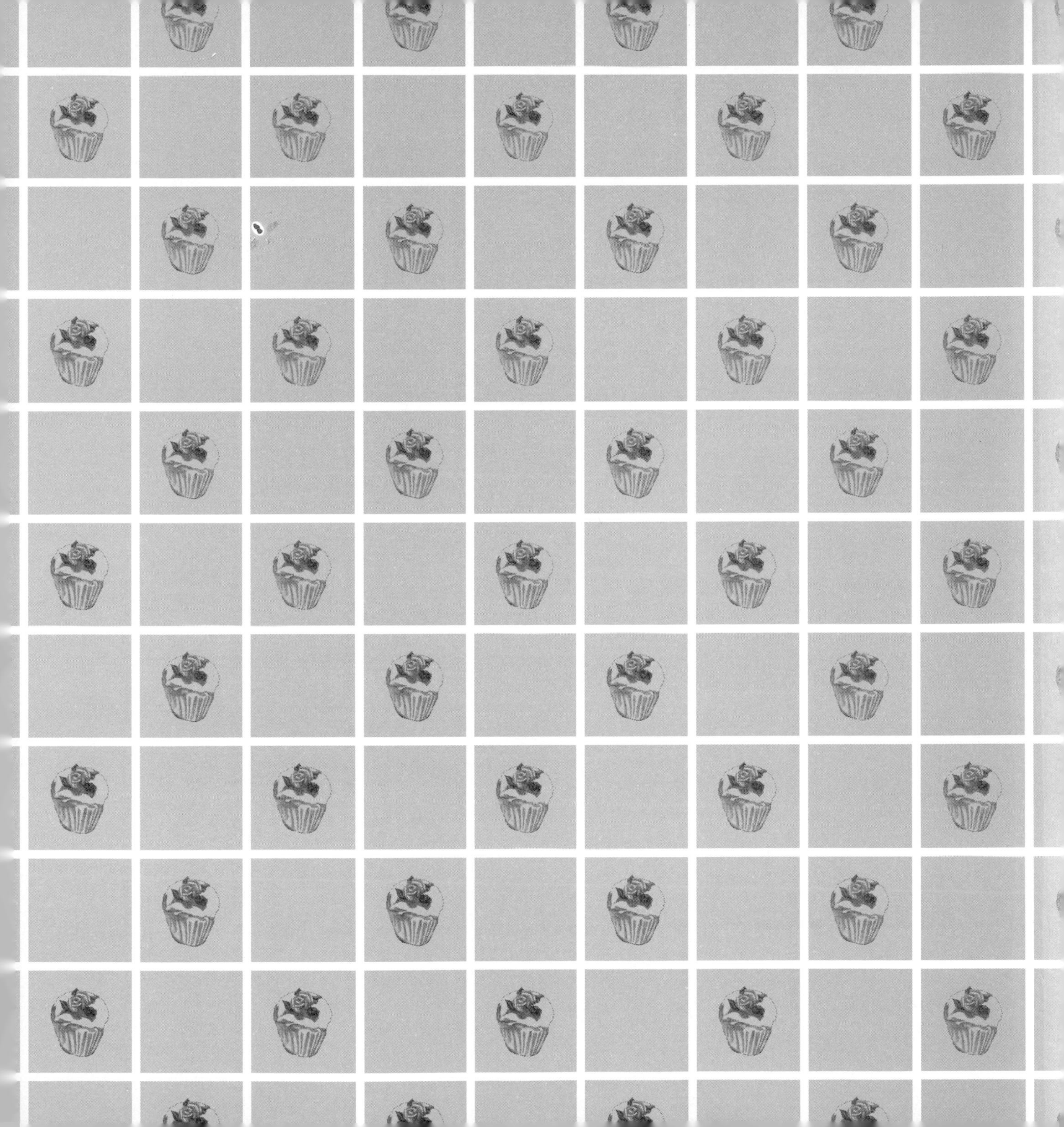

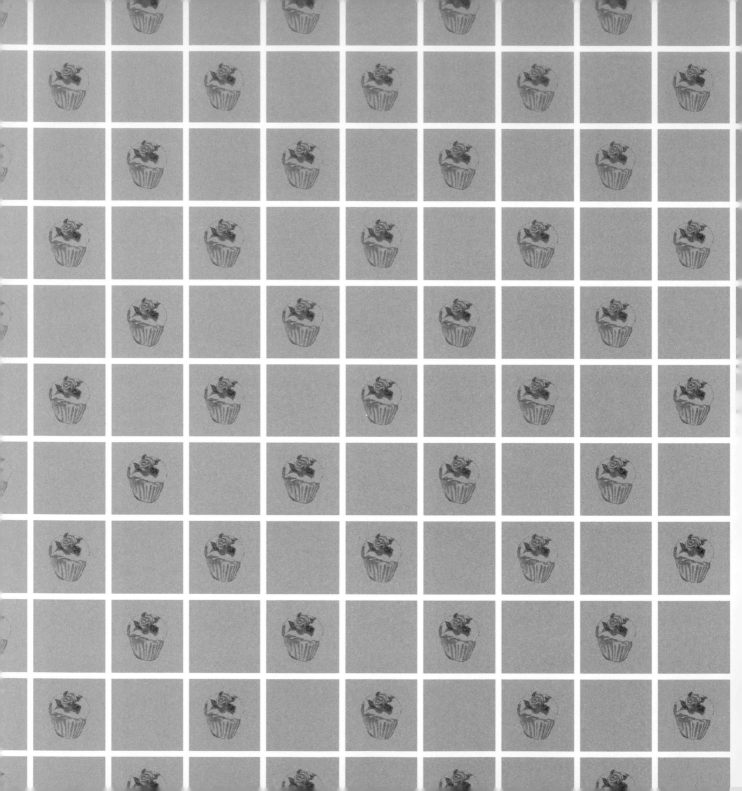

Dessert Baked Goods

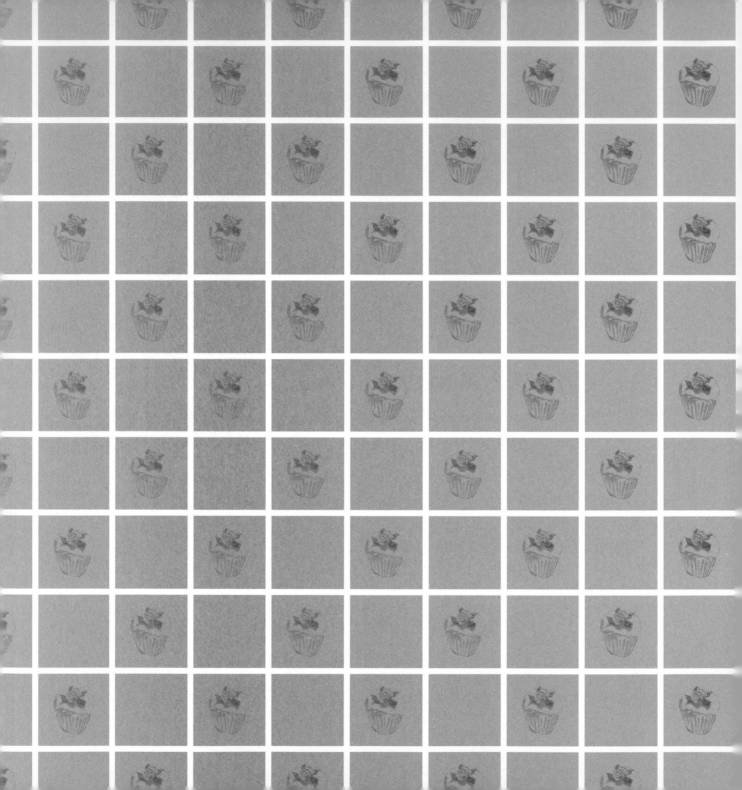

Gingerbread Cookies

We make these cookies in December for our annual cookie-decorating party, which supplies the cookies we hang in the window each year. This dough works well with cookie cutters—the traditional shapes as well as all the many interesting cookie cutter shapes currently available—and can also be used for building gingerbread houses. In addition, it is suitable for sculpting hand-shaped cookies. If your gingerbread cookies are intended more for show than consumption, add extra flour to the dough to toughen it up a bit. Baked and cooled, the cookies can be painted with a paste of confectioners' sugar, a little water, and food coloring. If you plan to hang them, don't forget to bore a small hole in your cookie before baking. A straw works well for this purpose.

1 POUND BUTTER	1/2 TEASPOON SALT
2 CUPS DARK BROWN SUGAR	1 1/2 TEASPOONS BAKING POWDER
1/2 CUP GRANULATED SUGAR	2 TEASPOONS GROUND CINNAMON
1 1/4 CUPS MOLASSES	2 TEASPOONS GROUND NUTMEG
2 EGGS	1/2 TEASPOON GROUND CLOVES
2 TEASPOONS BALSAMIC VINEGAR	2 TEASPOONS GROUND MACE
10 CUPS ALL-PURPOSE FLOUR	2 TEASPOONS POWDERED GINGER

Thoroughly grease a standard baking sheet. Preheat the oven to 400°F.

Cream together the butter and sugars. Add the molasses, then the eggs and vinegar. Sift together the rest of the ingredients. Mix everything together. Roll and cut into cookies. Place on sheet about an inch apart. Bake on the prepared baking sheet for 12 to 15 minutes, until lightly browned around the edges. Cool on a rack.

MAKES 7 TO 10 DOZEN, DEPENDING ON SIZE OF COOKIE CUTTER

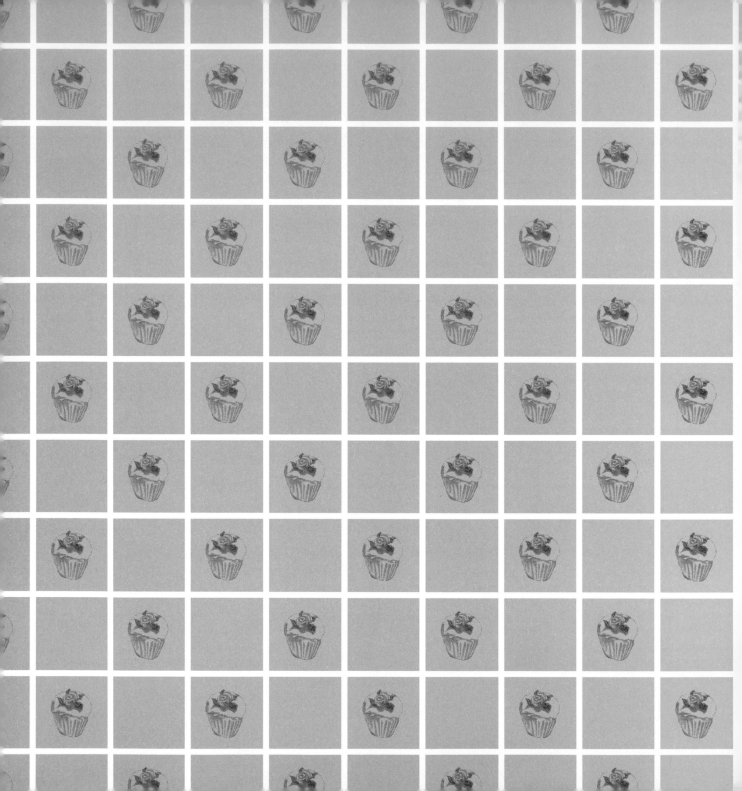

Oatmeal Cookies

½ POUND BUTTER

1 ½ CUPS DARK BROWN SUGAR

2 EGGS

1 TEASPOON PURE VANILLA EXTRACT

½ TEASPOON GRATED LEMON RIND

1 CUP ALL-PURPOSE FLOUR

¾ TEASPOON BAKING SODA

½ TEASPOON SALT

3 ½ CUPS ROLLED OATS

½ CUP DARK SEEDLESS RAISINS

Thoroughly grease a standard baking sheet. Preheat the oven to 375°F. Cream together the butter and the sugar. Add the eggs, vanilla, and lemon rind. Mix the flour, soda, and salt together and add the oats and raisins. Spoon out rounded teaspoonfuls of cookie dough onto the greased baking sheet.

Bake for about 12 minutes, until lightly browned.

MAKES ABOUT 18 COOKIES

Peanut Butter Cookies

1 CUP DARK BROWN SUGAR

1 CUP GRANULATED SUGAR

1/2 POUND BUTTER

1 1/2 POUNDS SMOOTH OR CHUNKY
    PEANUT BUTTER (NATURAL
    PREFERRED)

2 EGGS

1 TEASPOON PURE VANILLA EXTRACT

3 CUPS ALL-PURPOSE FLOUR

1 TEASPOON BAKING SODA

1 TEASPOON SALT

Thoroughly grease a baking sheet. Preheat the oven to 375°F. Cream together the sugars and the butter. Add the peanut butter, eggs, and vanilla. Sift the flour with the baking soda and salt. Add the flour mixture to the sugar mixture and combine. Scooping the dough with a tablespoon, drop balls of dough onto the greased cookie sheet. Press each one down once with the back of a fork. Space them about an inch apart so they have some room to spread. Bake for 12 to 15 minutes, until just beginning to brown. Cool on a rack and store airtight.

MAKES 2 1/2 DOZEN COOKIES

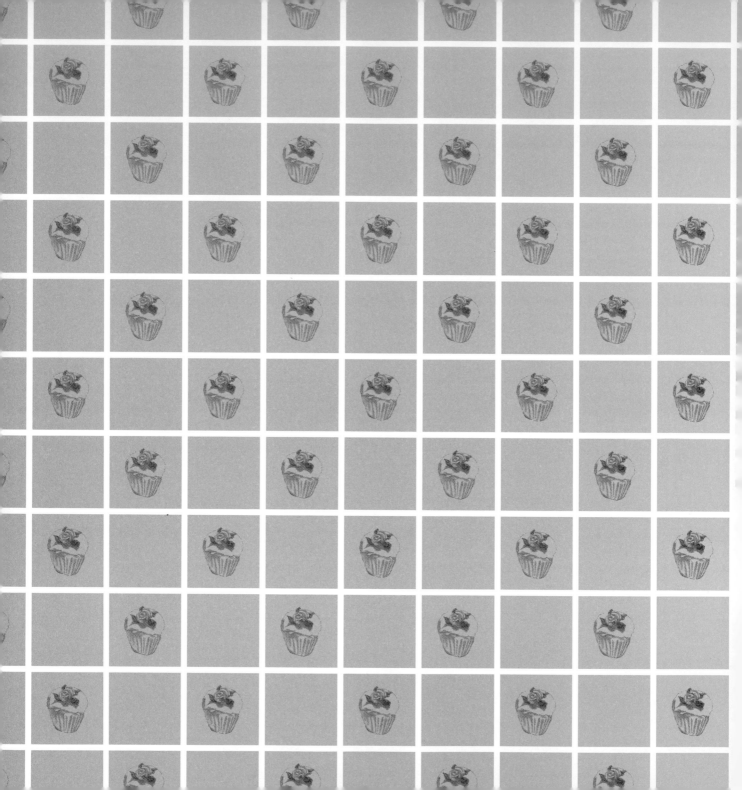

Chocolate Chip Cookies

½ POUND BUTTER

¾ CUP DARK BROWN SUGAR

¾ CUP GRANULATED SUGAR

2 EGGS

1 TEASPOON PURE VANILLA EXTRACT

2¼ CUPS ALL-PURPOSE FLOUR

1 TEASPOON BAKING POWDER

½ TEASPOON SALT

8 OUNCES REAL SEMISWEET
CHOCOLATE CHIPS

1 CUP SLIGHTLY CHOPPED WALNUTS

Thoroughly grease a baking sheet. Preheat the oven to 375°F. Cream the butter and sugars. Add the eggs and vanilla. Sift together the flour, baking powder, and salt. Stir the chocolate chips and walnuts into the flour mixture. Add the butter, egg, and sugar mixture and mix until completely combined. Scoop teaspoonfuls of dough onto the prepared baking sheet about 2 inches apart. Bake in batches about 12 minutes until lightly browned. Cool on a rack and store airtight.

MAKES 2½ TO 3 DOZEN COOKIES

Brownies

*Although it is not in our nature at the Café to be obsequious, I do think that these brownies
have managed to ingratiate themselves among the two major opposing brownie camps: those who really
want a piece of fudge (but feel less self-indulgent eating a brownie), and those who really don't want
something that sweet, and would probably be just as happy eating a nice piece of moist
chocolate cake if only they could find one.*

3 OUNCES (3 SQUARES) UNSWEETENED
  BAKING CHOCOLATE

½ POUND SWEET BUTTER

4 EGGS

½ CUP GRANULATED SUGAR

⅔ CUP DARK BROWN SUGAR

1 TEASPOON PURE VANILLA EXTRACT

3 CUPS ALL-PURPOSE FLOUR

1 TEASPOON BAKING POWDER

½ TEASPOON SALT

6 OUNCES REAL SEMISWEET
  CHOCOLATE CHIPS

½ CUP CHOPPED WALNUTS
  (OPTIONAL)

Preheat the oven to 350°F.

Melt the unsweetened chocolate into the butter (either in a double boiler or in the oven in
an ovenproof dish at 325°F, or microwave) and set it aside to cool. When cooled, add the eggs,
the sugars, and the vanilla. Sift the flour with the baking powder and salt and add the chocolate
chips. Combine the two mixtures and pour the batter into an 8 × 11-inch baking pan. Chopped
walnuts can be sprinkled on at this point if desired. Bake at 350°F for 25 to 35 minutes (remove
while still fudgy or slightly soft). Cool in the pan and cut into squares or rectangles.

MAKES 12 TO 16 BROWNIES

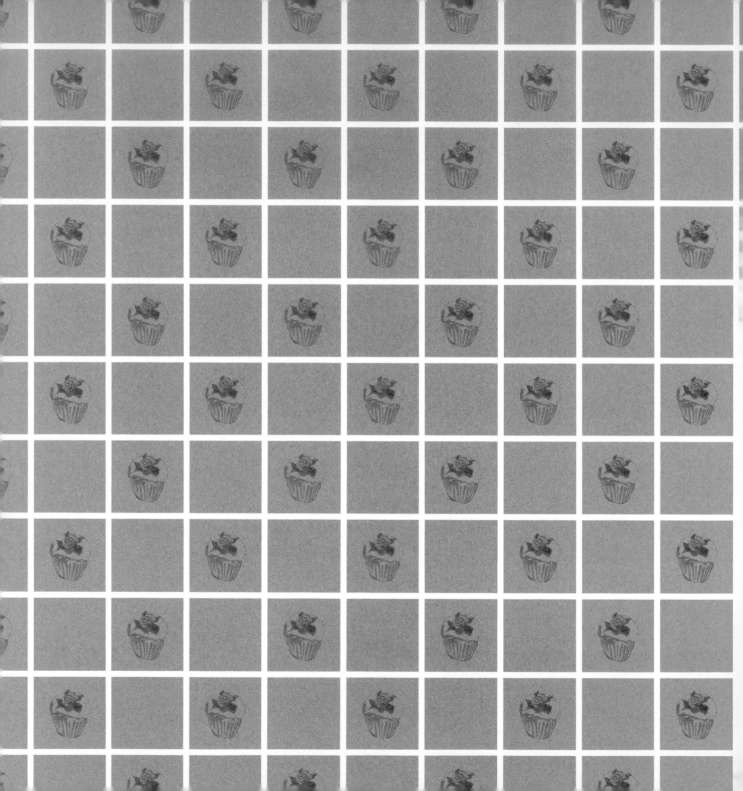

Fruitcake

*Our fruitcake is not meant for people who just don't like fruitcake at all, but it
is well received by those who like* some *fruitcakes. The cake part is not sticky or too sweet, and there are no
glacé cherries (red or green). This is not an all-natural-dried-fruit-no-sugar concoction either.
There is butter and brandy, candied peel, roasted hazelnuts, and some dried fruit, including natural dried
cherries. Most people feel fruitcake is an abomination, whereas ours is quite edible
(if you like fruitcake in the first place) and it keeps for several weeks.*

⅔ POUND CHOPPED CANDIED LEMON
   PEEL

⅔ POUND CHOPPED CANDIED ORANGE
   PEEL

¼ POUND CHOPPED CITRON

¼ POUND SEEDLESS DARK RAISINS

⅓ POUND SULTANAS OR GOLDEN
   RAISINS

⅓ POUND CURRANTS

½ POUND DRIED CHERRIES (NOT
   CANDIED)

¼ POUND DRIED CRANBERRIES
   (NOT CANDIED)

¼ POUND CHOPPED CANDIED
   PINEAPPLE

1½ CUPS BRANDY

2 POUNDS HAZELNUTS OR USE
   1 POUND HAZELNUTS AND 1 POUND
   ALMONDS

1 POUND BUTTER

2 CUPS SUGAR

1 CUP BROWN SUGAR

2 TABLESPOONS PURE VANILLA
   EXTRACT

12 EGGS

1 TEASPOON ORANGE OIL OR
   1 TABLESPOON GRATED ORANGE PEEL

1 CUP BREWED COFFEE

5 CUPS FLOUR

1½ TABLESPOONS BAKING POWDER

2 TEASPOONS GROUND NUTMEG

1 TEASPOON GROUND CINNAMON

1 TEASPOON POWDERED GINGER

½ TEASPOON SALT

CRYSTALLIZED GINGER, SLIVERED, FOR
   SPRINKLING LOAVES

Assemble the candied peels, citron, raisins, currants, dried cherries and cranberries, and 1 cup of the brandy in a large bowl (glass, ceramic, or plastic, but not metal).

Allow to sit at least 5 hours, or as long as overnight, mixing occasionally.

Roast the nuts in oven at 325° for 15 to 25 minutes, until lightly browned. After they have cooled slightly, rub them between your fingers to remove the skins. Put them in a food processor for a brief pulse or two, to chop *just slightly* (halved to quartered). Set aside. When the fruit is ready, mix the butter and sugars together.

Add to this the vanilla, eggs, orange oil, coffee, and the remaining ½ cup brandy. Set aside.

Mix first, then toss over the fruit, the flour, baking powder, nutmeg, cinnamon, ginger, and salt.

Toss well, then add the chopped nuts and mix again. Add the butter, sugar, and egg mixture to the fruit/flour mixture. Thoroughly grease four 7-inch loaf pans. Pour the batter into the prepared pans, filling them about three-quarters full. Top each loaf with slivers of crystallized ginger.

Bake in a preheated oven at 325°F for 1¼ to 1½ hours.

Remove from pans, allow to cool, and wrap well to keep moist after baking. Some additional brandy can be poured or brushed over the tops before wrapping, and again later on, if desired.

4 LOAVES

Strawberry Shortcake

The Café's debut took place during the annual Ninth Avenue Food Festival in 1988 where we sold individual portions of strawberry shortcake. Flat after flat of beautiful ripe strawberries were washed and sliced and sprinkled with sugar to exude their own syrup. We baked batch after batch of rich biscuits, which were split, filled with sliced fresh berries, and covered in barely sweetened, fresh-whipped heavy cream. They were served and consumed nearly as soon as they were assembled. We recommend you do the same — try to serve your strawberry shortcake while the biscuits are still warm. The simplest of desserts, this biscuit-style shortcake is both easily made and happily devoured by almost everyone.

1 QUART RIPE STRAWBERRIES, WASHED, HULLED, AND SLICED

1/3 CUP PLUS 2 TABLESPOONS SUGAR

3 CUPS ALL-PURPOSE FLOUR

1 TABLESPOON BAKING POWDER

3/4 TEASPOON SALT

6 OUNCES COLD BUTTER (1 1/2 STICKS), CUT UP (PLUS 2 OUNCES, OPTIONAL)

3/4 CUP WHOLE MILK OR BUTTERMILK*

1 PINT HEAVY CREAM

Combine the strawberries with 1/3 cup sugar and set aside.

Butter a baking sheet. Preheat the oven to 400°F. Combine the flour, baking powder, and salt. Rub in by hand, or use a pastry blade to cut in the cold butter. Add the milk and form 1 large round biscuit, or roll out the dough to about 1 1/2 inches thick and cut individual biscuits with a biscuit cutter. Place about 2 inches apart on the prepared baking sheet and bake about 12 minutes for individual biscuits and 20 to 25 minutes for a large one until slightly browned.

Beat the heavy cream with the remaining 2 tablespoons of sugar until it holds in soft peaks. For one large shortcake: Slice the shortcake in half horizontally (optional: butter slightly). Cover with half the strawberries and top with the other half of the shortcake. Cover with the rest of the berries, top with whipped cream, and serve. For individual shortcakes: Distribute half the strawberries evenly over the halved biscuits, then top the biscuits with the remaining berries and cream.

MAKES 6 TO 8 SERVINGS

*If using buttermilk, reduce baking powder to 2 teaspoons and add ⅔ teaspoon baking soda.

PIES

ON MAKING PIE

I grew up watching my Aunt Hadi put together pies with the sort of crisp efficiency with which some people fold their laundry. And the truth is, making a pie does not need to be looked upon as a major undertaking. If you want to make a pie, you can. Unfortunately, a lot of people are scared of pie-making.

If you are in the makes-pie-crust-already group, skip this whole section. There is nothing really special in our crust recipe except that we use it commercially. Although my aunt uses lard, we use vegetable shortening—with butter added for taste—so that vegetarians can partake in good conscience.

For those of you who think you can't make pie, the first thing you need to do is forget the idea that some people are born pie makers. (I've yet to see a baby make a nice flaky pie crust.) And the cold hands thing. My hands are unusually cold, and I can mess up a crust as easily as the next person. And although perhaps you *can* use luck or intuition to make a pie, you might better conserve those commodities for important things like choosing lotto numbers. Go slowly and pay attention.

Now, in the world of pie-crust-making, cold hands are not a bad thing, but the main thing is not to heat up or overwork the dough. Why would you overwork the dough? Because you are thinking about what it will look like. Don't. Pie is to eat. A good-looking pie will just happen with experience. Don't try to obtain all that experience with the same poor pie crust.

Aim for character and personality in your pie as opposed to uniformity. Why would you want your pie to look like someone else's, anyway? Would you want your children to look like someone else made them?

What not overworking the crust means is this—treat the dough gently. Roll it out only once if possible. Fix the edge with the lightest touch you can. Less is more here, that's all. When rolling dough, adding too much water or too much extra flour toughens the crust. Durability in a pie crust is not desirable. You're not making an ashtray. If a bit falls off the edge it's no cause to panic.

Pie Crust Dough

5 TABLESPOONS BUTTER (2 ½ OUNCES)

⅔ CUP SOLID VEGETABLE
    SHORTENING

2 ½ CUPS ALL-PURPOSE FLOUR

1 ¼ TEASPOONS SALT

½ CUP COLD WATER

Cut up the butter and vegetable shortening (so they're about the size of diced vegetables) and let them sit loosely arranged on a plate in the freezer while you prepare your pie filling. (Recipes for fillings follow.)

When you're ready to go back to your crust: Mix together the flour and salt. Add the cold shortening and butter and work everything together with your fingertips quickly so as not to melt the shortening. Try not to overwork the dough. When the mixture has the texture of very coarsely ground whole wheat flour or cornmeal, add just enough cold water so that it is possible to roll it out. This can vary a bit depending on humidity in the room and your flour, so start with ¾ cup and add just what you feel you need to be able to roll out the dough.

Flour a clean surface, divide the dough in half, and with a floured rolling pin or a straight-sided bottle, roll each piece out to about ⅛-inch thick. Use the long edge of a spatula to help move the crust to the pie plate. If it breaks a bit don't worry, any patching won't show anyway. Crimp the edges with your fingers, evening out the crust as you go.

If you're very short of counter space you can make a bottom crust without rolling it out. Just distribute the loose dough into the pie plate as evenly as you can and press it gently into the sides—if it holds together, don't worry what it looks like; once the pie is filled the inside of the crust won't be visible. Finish the edges as above, and fill.

MAKES ENOUGH DOUGH FOR ONE 10-INCH, 2-CRUST PIE

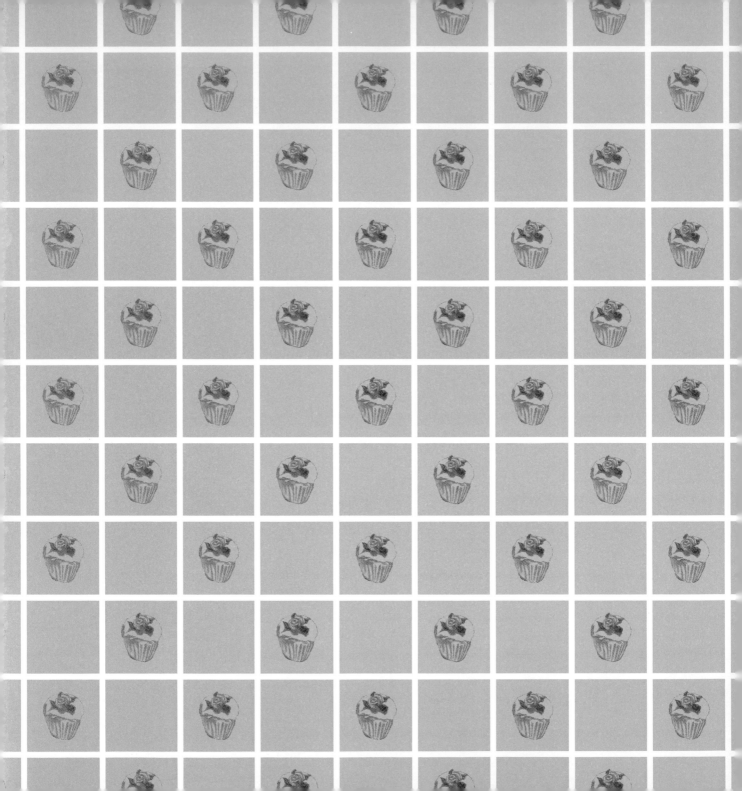

Apple Pie

Filling

4 POUNDS APPLES SUCH AS GOLDEN
  DELICIOUS, MCINTOSH, ROME, OR
  GRANNY SMITH (ABOUT 6 CUPS
  PEELED AND SLICED)

2 TABLESPOONS GRANULATED SUGAR

¼ CUP DARK BROWN SUGAR

1 ½ TO 2 TABLESPOONS
  ALL-PURPOSE FLOUR

¼ TEASPOON GROUND MACE

1 TEASPOON GROUND CINNAMON

¼ TEASPOON GROUND CLOVES

¼ TEASPOON POWDERED GINGER

¼ TEASPOON GROUND NUTMEG

PINCH OF SALT

2 TO 3 TABLESPOONS MELTED BUTTER

1 RECIPE PIE CRUST DOUGH
  (PAGE 97)

Preheat the oven to 400°F.

Peel, core, and slice the apples. Add all the remaining filling ingredients and mix well. Place the mixture into an unbaked 10-inch pie shell. Cover with the top crust, crimp the edges together, and slash steam vents into the top with a knife or prick with a fork. Place on the middle shelf of the preheated oven and bake 10 minutes. Turn the oven temperature down to 350°F and bake 30 to 35 minutes longer. To test for doneness, pierce apples through a steam vent. The top should be nicely browned.

MAKES 6 TO 10 SERVINGS

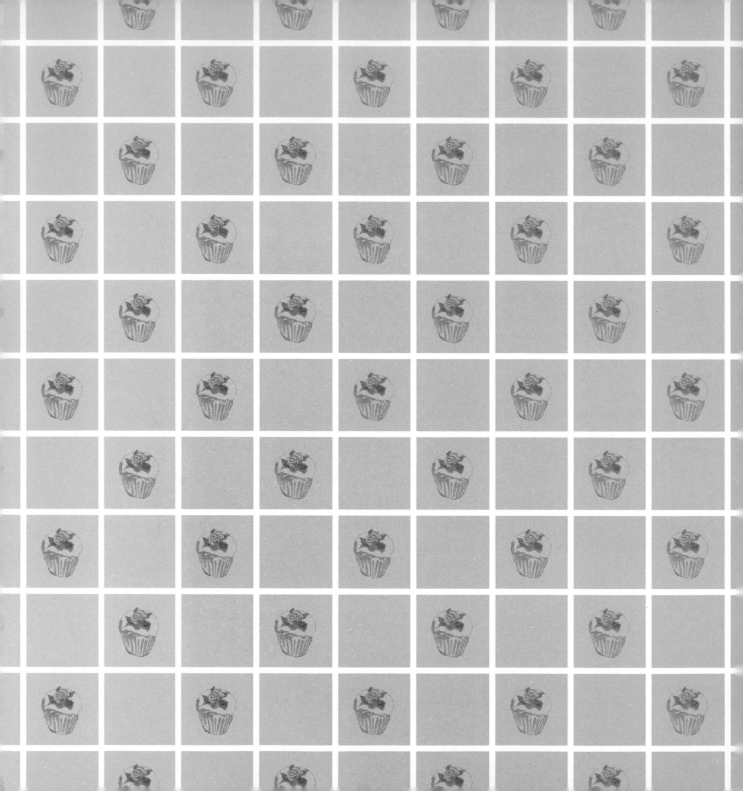

Pumpkin Pie

This is a very rich pie, not too spicy or sweet.

Filling

4 EGGS

1/2 CUP DARK BROWN SUGAR

1/4 CUP GRANULATED SUGAR

1 POUND UNSWEETENED CANNED
   PUMPKIN

1/2 TEASPOON SALT

1 TEASPOON GROUND CINNAMON

1/2 TEASPOON POWDERED GINGER

1/2 TEASPOON GROUND ALLSPICE

1/4 TEASPOON GROUND MACE

1/2 TEASPOON GROUND NUTMEG

2 TABLESPOONS MELTED BUTTER

1/2 CUP HEAVY CREAM*

1/2 CUP LIGHT CREAM*

1/2 RECIPE PIE CRUST DOUGH
   (PAGE 97)

Preheat the oven to 325°F.

Combine all the filling ingredients in the order given, making certain that the spices are well distributed. Pour the filling into a prepared unbaked 10-inch pie shell and bake for about 30 to 35 minutes, until set. You can test it with a knife for doneness, as you would a custard. (If the knife blade comes out clean, it's ready to take out). The crust edges should be slightly browned as well. Cool and, if not eating the pie within 4 hours, store it, wrapped airtight, in the refrigerator.

MAKES 6 TO 8 SERVINGS

*For either or both of these you can substitute half and half, milk, or even part skim milk. The result will be less rich, but it will set and be just as pie-like. Just use 1 cup total.

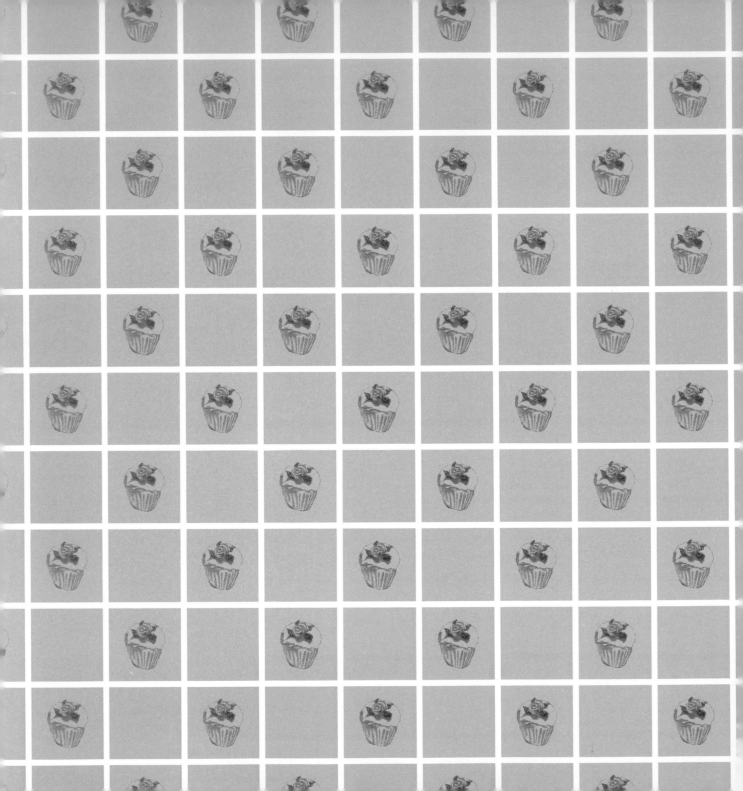

Blueberry Pie

Filling

1 QUART BLUEBERRIES

3 TABLESPOONS PLUS 1 TEASPOON
TAPIOCA

1/2 TO 2/3 CUP GRANULATED SUGAR
(DEPENDING ON BERRY TARTNESS)

JUICE OF 1/2 LEMON

1/2 TEASPOON GROUND NUTMEG

1 RECIPE PIE CRUST DOUGH
(PAGE 97)

Preheat the oven to 375°F.

Wash, clean, and pick over the berries, removing any stems or rotten berries. Add all the remaining filling ingredients and allow the mixture to sit at least 15 minutes. Then pour the filling mixture into an unbaked 10-inch pie shell and top with a lattice crust. To make the lattice crust, roll out the dough that you have reserved for the top crust onto a well-floured surface to a 3/16-inch thickness (a little less than a quarter of an inch). The shape is not important, except that it should be at least eleven inches wide at the center and at least 12 inches long. With a knife cut the dough in strips 3/4 inches wide. Your longest piece should be at least 11 inches. Place the filled pie in front of you. Imagine it is a map and the edge farthest from you is north, closest to you south, to the right east, and to the left west. Use your longest strips first, saving the shortest ones for last when you're looking to span short distances. To begin, take the longest strip and lay it over the pie near the center north to south. Take the next longest piece and lay it across west to east so it crosses near the center. Place the third strip parallel to the first strip leaving about 1/2 inch between them. (The third strip will cross over the second.) Your fourth strip will run west to east: using the next longest strip lay it down either above or below the second strip, lifting the first strip up to allow this fourth strip to lie under the first and over the third strip. Continue weaving in this manner, working out from the center one strand to the east, one to the north, next to the west, next to the south, lifting only every other strip and letting it lay over the others until the pie is covered with a woven lattice. Use any extra dough at the edge to crimp an edge which should be high enough to help contain any expansion of the filling that occurs during baking. Bake for 25 to 35 minutes, until browned and bubbly. (Unless you like the feeling of having the top of your mouth peel off, wait until it's cooled a bit before consuming it.)

MAKES 6 TO 8 SERVINGS

Cherry Pie

1 QUART SOUR CHERRIES IN JUICE
(CANNED, FROZEN, OR BOTTLED)

¼ CUP TAPIOCA

⅔ CUP GRANULATED SUGAR
(OPTIONAL)

1 RECIPE PIE CRUST DOUGH
(PAGE 97)

Combine the cherries and tapioca in a saucepan and allow the mixture to sit for 10 minutes, then bring to a boil over medium heat, reduce the heat, and simmer for about 5 minutes. Preheat the oven to 375°F.

Depending on whether or not your cherries were packed with sugar, you may wish to add sugar. Taste them first to see if they are sweet enough. If not, add up to ⅔ cup of granulated sugar. Cool slightly, then pour into an unbaked 10-inch pie shell and cover with a lattice crust (see Blueberry Pie recipe, page 103). Bake about 35 minutes, until the crust is browned.

MAKES 6 TO 8 SERVINGS

Pecan Pie

Filling

5 EGGS

1 ¼ CUPS KARO SYRUP

¼ CUP REAL MAPLE SYRUP

1 TEASPOON PURE VANILLA EXTRACT

¼ CUP MELTED BUTTER

¼ TEASPOON SALT

2 TABLESPOONS BOURBON WHISKEY

2 CUPS PECAN HALVES

½ RECIPE PIE CRUST DOUGH
  (PAGE 97)

Preheat the oven to 400°F.

Mix together all the filling ingredients except the pecans. Arrange the pecans in the bottom of a 10-inch unbaked pie shell, and pour the filling over them. Bake for 7 minutes, then reduce the oven temperature to 350°F and continue baking until set but still soft, about 25 to 30 minutes more.

MAKES 6 TO 10 SERVINGS

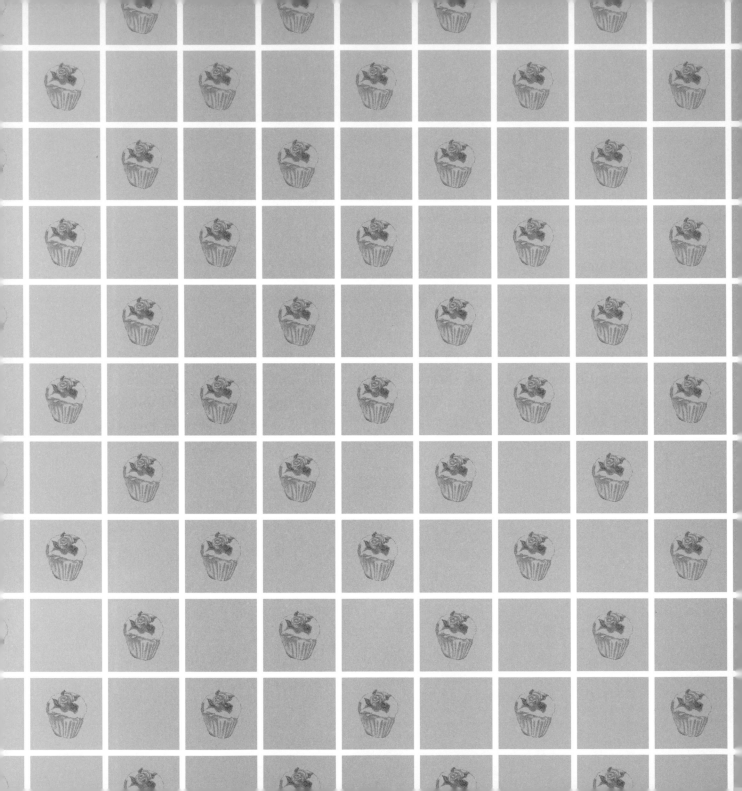

Sweet Potato Pie

1/2 TEASPOON GROUND MACE

1/2 TEASPOON GROUND CINNAMON

3/4 CUP BROWN SUGAR

2 3/4 CUPS COOKED, PEELED, AND RICED
 SWEET POTATO (ABOUT 3 POUNDS
 POTATOES)

4 EGGS

1 TEASPOON PURE VANILLA EXTRACT

1 1/2 CUPS LIGHT CREAM*

1/2 RECIPE PIE CRUST DOUGH
 (PAGE 97)

Preheat the oven to 400°F.

Mix the spices and brown sugar thoroughly into the sweet potatoes and add the eggs, one at a time, until well blended. Add the vanilla and the cream, blending well. Pour into a crimped, unbaked 10-inch pie crust. Bake 10 minutes at 400°F then reduce the heat to 350°F and bake an additional 20 to 30 minutes. Insert a knife into center of pie—if it comes out clean, the pie is ready to take out.

MAKES ONE 10-INCH PIE

*You can substitute half and half, whole milk, skim milk, or part whole and part skim for the cream.

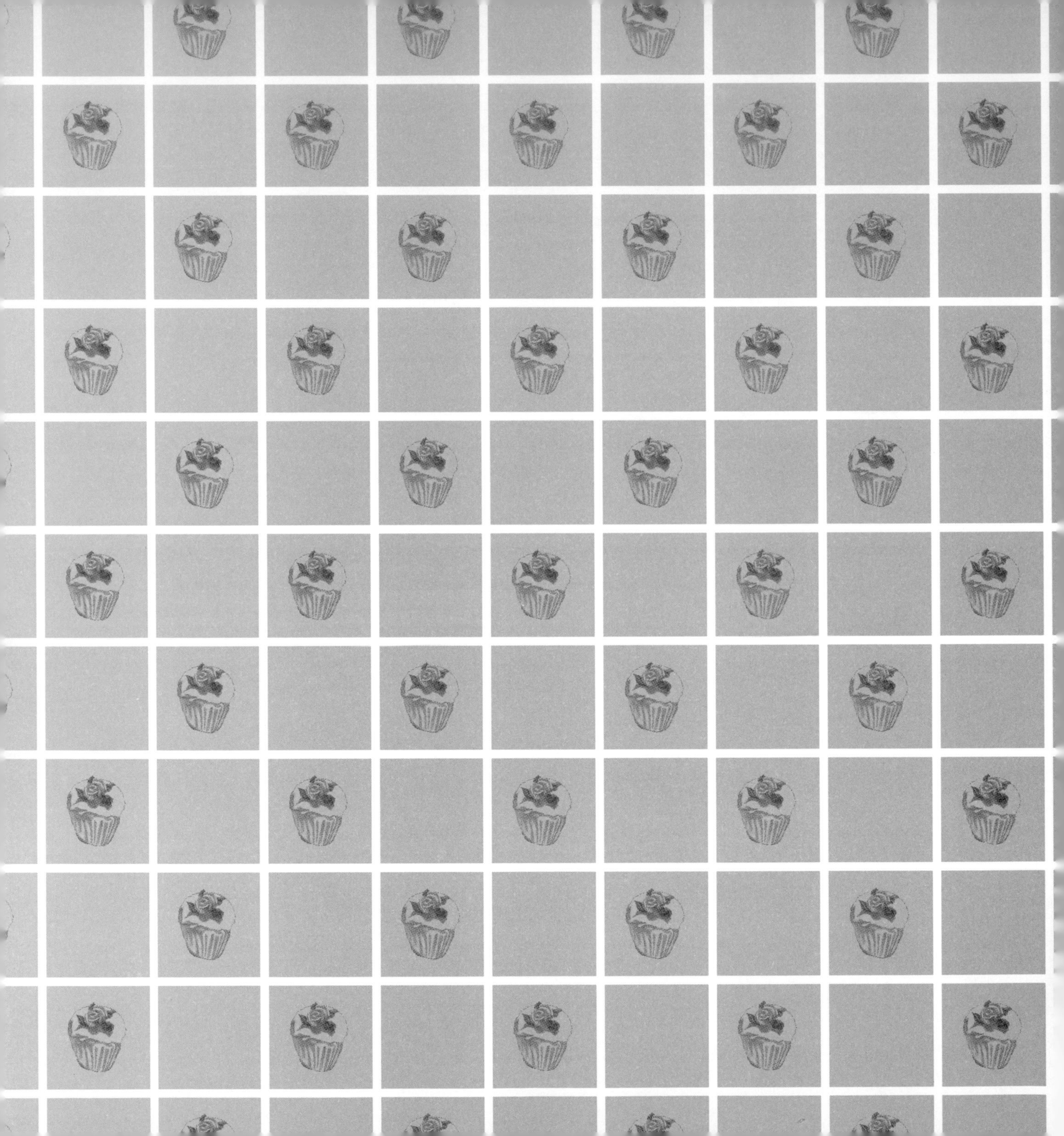

Rhubarb Cream Pie

Traditionally, this is known as rhubarb cream pie because of the eggs. It contains no cream.

1 ½ CUPS SUGAR

3 TABLESPOONS FLOUR

½ TEASPOON NUTMEG

1 TABLESPOON BUTTER

2 EGGS, WELL BEATEN

3 CUPS CHOPPED RHUBARB
(NOT TOO FINE)

1 RECIPE PIE CRUST DOUGH
(PAGE 97)

Mix first five ingredients together well. Pour over 3 cups rhubarb in an uncooked 9-inch pie shell. Top with lattice crust. Bake at 450°F for 10 minutes, then turn down to 350°F for 30 minutes more.

MAKES ONE 9-INCH PIE

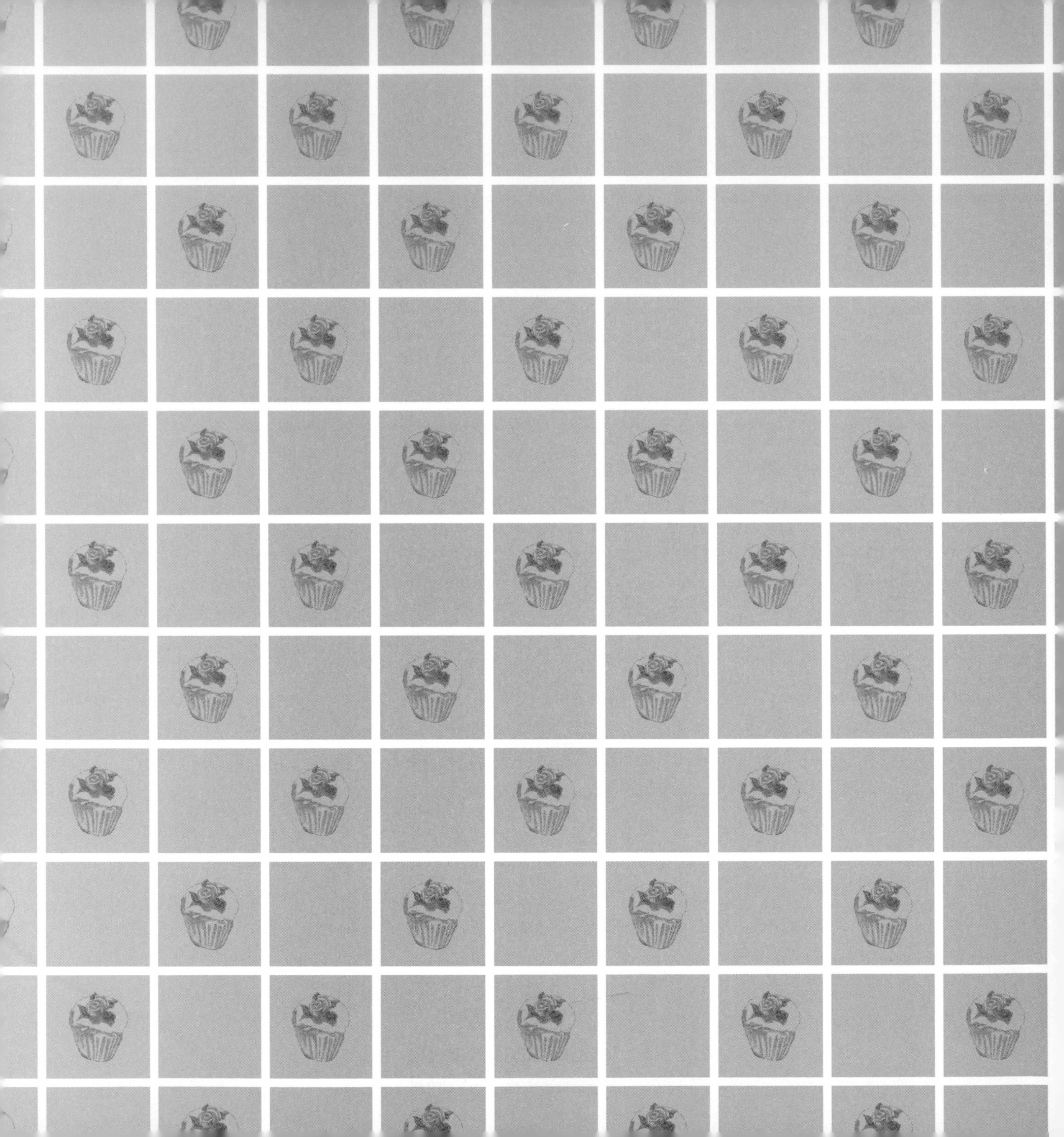

Mincemeat Pie

Filling

2 CUPS APPLES SUCH AS GOLDEN
   DELICIOUS, MCINTOSH, ROME, OR
   GRANNY SMITH (PEELED, CORED, AND
   CHOPPED INTO MEDIUM CHUNKS)

1/2 CUP DARK BROWN SUGAR

1 CUP FRUIT JUICE

1/4 POUND CANDIED LEMON PEEL

4 TABLESPOONS BUTTER

1/4 POUND CANDIED ORANGE PEEL

1 TO 2 CUPS WALNUTS

1 CUP SOUR CHERRIES AND THEIR
   JUICE

1 CUP CURRANTS

1/2 CUP DARK SEEDLESS RAISINS

1 CUP GOLDEN RAISINS

1/2 TEASPOON GROUND CINNAMON

1 TEASPOON GROUND NUTMEG

1 TEASPOON GROUND ALLSPICE

1/2 TEASPOON GROUND CLOVES

1/2 TEASPOON GROUND CORIANDER

1/4 TEASPOON SALT

1/2 TEASPOON PEPPER

1/2 TEASPOON POWDERED GINGER

3 TABLESPOONS BRANDY

2 RECIPES PIE CRUST DOUGH
   (PAGE 97)

Combine all the filling ingredients except the brandy in a pot, and cook over medium heat for 1 hour. Remove from the heat, stir in the brandy, and refrigerate in a ceramic, plastic, or glass (not metal) bowl for at least 24 hours or until ready to use.

Preheat the oven to 375°F. Pour the mincemeat into two unbaked 9-inch pie shells. Cover with the top crusts and bake for 40 minutes, until the crust is browned.

MAKES 8 TO 10 SERVINGS PER PIE

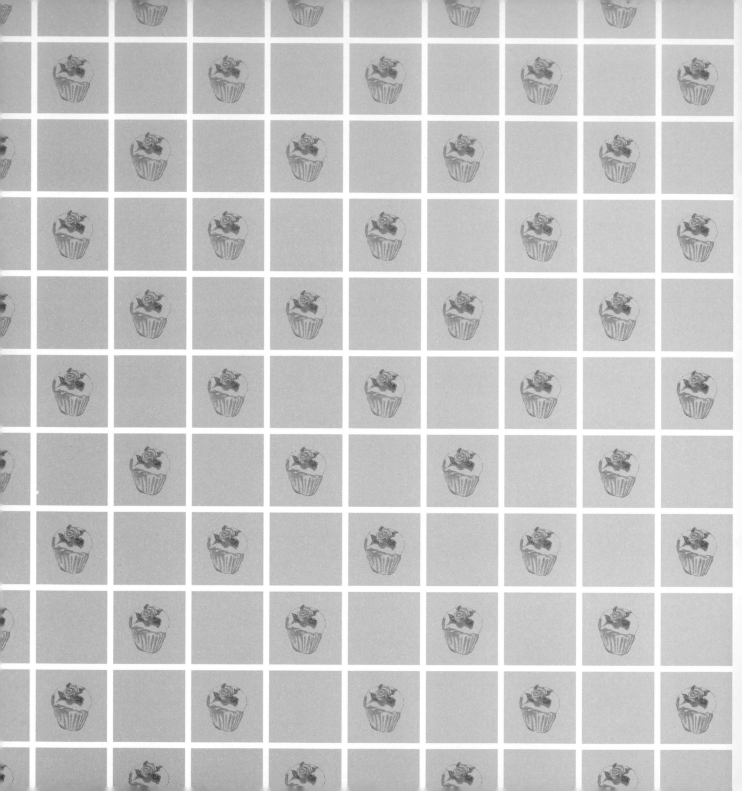

Cakes

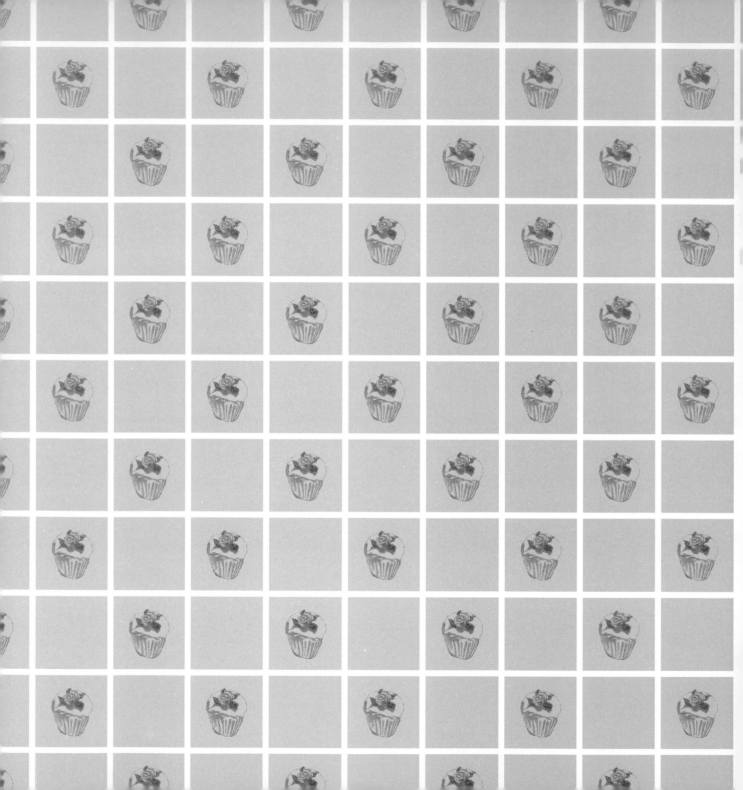

INTRODUCTION

$\mathcal{H}$aving my life enveloped in butter cream is not something I set out to do. (I thought Michael and I were going to reintroduce fresh, made-from-scratch doughnuts to New York City.) So I can appreciate that there will be readers who do not envision a butter cream bath on their own horizon. I have tried, however, to consider the interests of both those who have never done any cake decorating before, and those who may be experienced decorators—in butter cream or in another medium—and are looking for either technical advice (e.g., Which tip works best for poinsettias?) or inspiration (e.g., What can I put on my nephew's cake?).

Decorators who have worked with other frostings, such as royal icing, will discover that butter cream is much more flexible and thus less likely to break. Real butter cream is as soft, or softer, than other frostings, but holds its shape. (It also tastes good—unless you don't happen to like butter.)

While some of the material in this section, particularly about frosting and inscribing, may seem geared to those who are already doing a lot of decorating (or have a perfectionist bent), the beginner and the less ambitious should not be put off. Most people, rightly, expect dessert to be eaten, not to be viewed as an *objet d'art*.

A few words about the organization of this section should help users of varying intent find their way: Recipes for our cakes, and instructions for preparing butter cream, follow this introduction. After the recipes, I've inserted a section on the equipment you'll need for frosting, inscribing, and decorating. Unless you've used butter cream before, it is probably a good idea to look over the equipment section before proceeding, even if you simply wish to bake and frost your cake, or perhaps add an inscription. Basting (or frosting) cakes is covered after equipment, followed by a section on how to write on cakes. Then we get to decorating, with a section on forming flowers with butter cream.

I have used roses as something of a teaching example—in part because they are popular on cakes and everyone knows pretty much what a rose looks like, and in part because roses take enough dexterity that by the time you can handle butter cream skillfully enough to do a respectable rose, you should find most other flowers relatively easy to make. (Peonies are included at the end of the roses section as their construction is very similar.)

Roses come in an abundant assortment of colors, so within the section on roses/peonies I've included formulas for mixing up a large assortment of colors, which will be of use with many other flowers as well. After the instruction for forming each flower, I've included color formulas for the most common varieties of that flower. (If there's a color you can't find under another flower heading, try the roses/peonies section.) I will confess that our own method of creating colored butter cream is not nearly so precise as what's given here (you won't find anyone at the Café counting out drops) but again, I've tried to consider varying levels of both experience and adventuresomeness.

Some general comments on how leaves help a cake are included in the rose section as well, although, again, within the section on each of the other flowers covered, I've given suggestions for creating the leaves for that particular flower.

You don't, of course, have to begin decorating by learning to make roses. If you are less interested in decorating in general than you are in getting a *particular* cake decorated, you might choose to forgo roses for now and try sunflowers or daisies, which, along with violets, are probably the easiest flowers to make in butter cream. (Or, not trying to avoid difficulty, you might just really like sunflowers, daisies, and violets.)

In the section on forming other flowers with butter cream, I've covered varieties other than roses and peonies. I have grouped together flowers that are fashioned similarly, so that, for instance, when you've got the hang of making one sort of three-dimensional flower with petals that radiate from the center such as zinnias, it should seem like a natural extension to go on to another, such as dahlias. Instructions for a couple of seasonal cake elements are included here as well.

After the flower sections, I've included some thoughts on composition, for those who'd like some advice on what to do with these flowers they've just mastered.

Picture cakes are covered in the next section, including suggestions for what to put on children's cakes (considering your level of experience and the age of the child) and some general comments on picture cakes for adults.

You can, in effect, paint with butter cream. One of the ways that butter cream is different (and in my mind, better) than other frostings is in the quality of its colors, which have a depth, a translucent quality, almost like oil paint or glaze. Cold butter cream looks matt, but not a cold stone dead matt like royal icings.

I finish up with a section on putting together and decorating wedding cakes of two and three tiers. (I haven't gone any higher here, under the assumption that anyone making a wedding cake for 200 people or more should really know what they are doing; I don't want any toppled four-tiered cakes on my conscience.)

The chocolate cake is also good just plain.

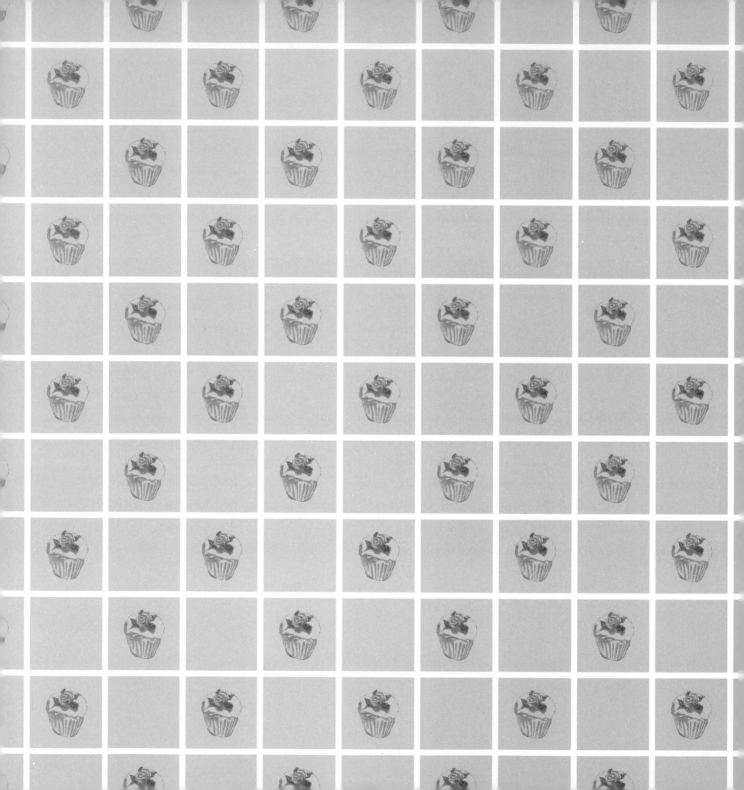

Cupcake Café Vanilla Cake

9 EGGS

¾ POUND BUTTER

3 CUPS SUGAR

1 ½ TEASPOONS PURE VANILLA
  EXTRACT

3 CUPS PASTRY FLOUR

1 ½ TEASPOONS BAKING POWDER

¾ TEASPOON BAKING SODA

½ TEASPOON SALT

1 ½ CUPS BUTTERMILK

Thoroughly butter two 8- or 9-inch round cake pans. (For hints on no-stick pan preparation, see the footnote for the Chocolate Cake recipe on page 123.) Preheat the oven to 350°F.

Carefully separate the eggs, making sure not to get any yolk in the whites. If you're not sure you can do this (some poorer quality eggs have very easily broken yolks) crack each egg separately over a cup adding only those whites that are free of yolk. (The alternate situation, getting some of the egg white in with the yolks, is not a problem.) Put the whites aside at room temperature to be beaten later.

Cream the butter and sugar together. Beat in the egg yolks, add the vanilla, and set aside.

Sift together the cake flour, baking powder, baking soda, and salt. Beat the egg whites until they are fluffy (they should just hold their shape), but not at all dry. Mix the dry ingredients and buttermilk alternately into the egg and butter mixture. Do *not* overbeat. Then gently fold in the egg whites.

Fill your buttered, prepared pans about two-thirds full. Bake in the preheated oven for 35 to 40 minutes. You can test for doneness by inserting a straw or cake tester into the center of each cake. If it comes out clean (i.e., without any batter sticking to it) the cake is done and should be removed from the oven. Cakes can also be tested for doneness by pressing them gently in the center. If they have a slightly springy feel, they are ready to come out.

MAKES TWO 8- OR 9-INCH CAKE LAYERS

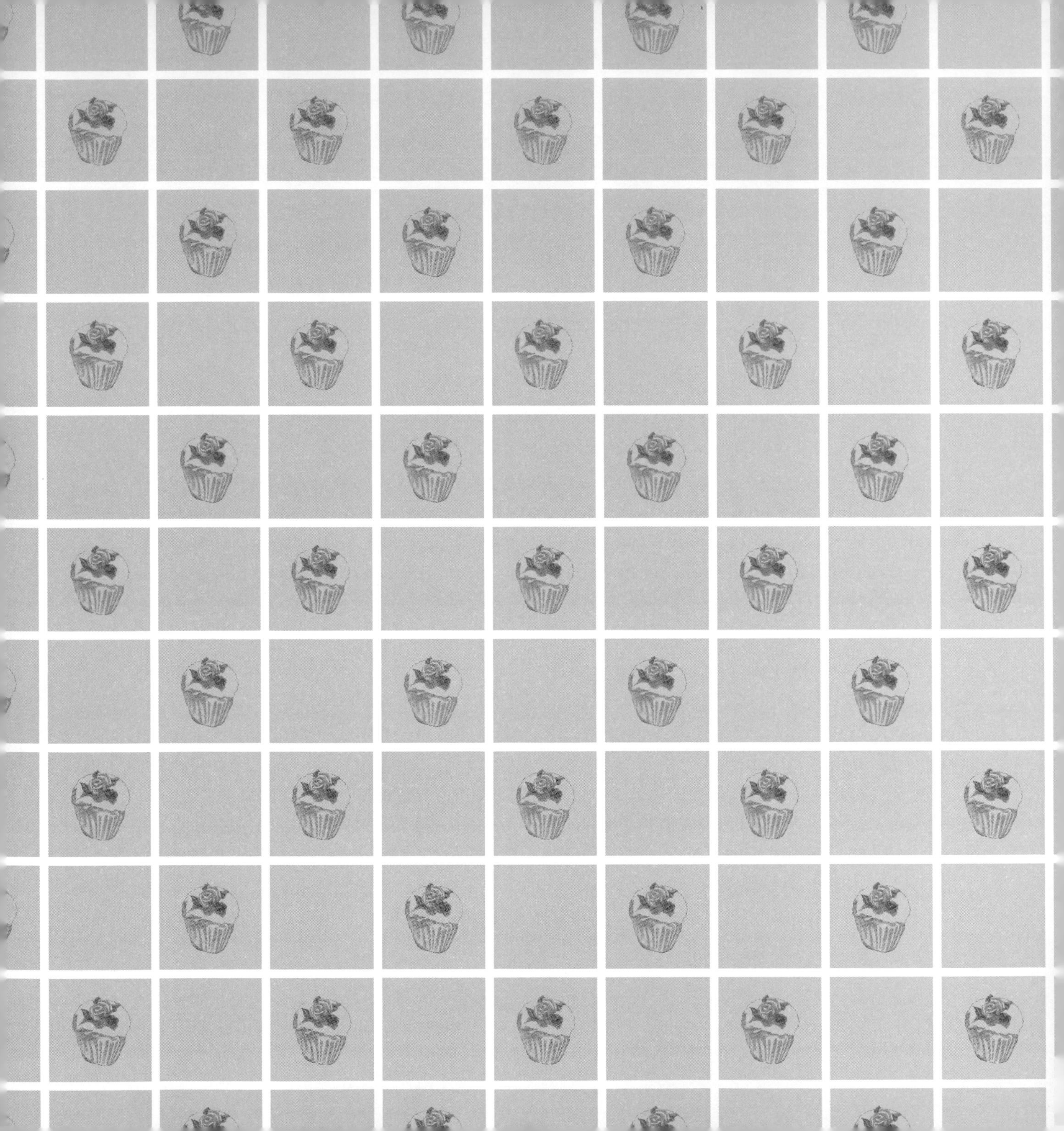

Cupcake Café Chocolate Cake

1 POUND BUTTER

2⅓ CUPS GRANULATED SUGAR

⅔ CUP DARK BROWN SUGAR

7 EGGS

6 OUNCES BAKER'S UNSWEETENED
CHOCOLATE

4½ CUPS PASTRY FLOUR

1 TEASPOON BAKING POWDER

2 TEASPOONS BAKING SODA

1 TEASPOON SALT

⅔ CUP COCOA

2 TEASPOONS PURE VANILLA EXTRACT

2⅓ CUPS BUTTERMILK

Butter two 10-inch round layer cake pans and dust them with cocoa.* Preheat the oven to 350°F.

Cream together the butter, granulated sugar, and brown sugar. Beat in the eggs, then melt the chocolate in a double boiler over simmering water and allow it to cool.

Sift together the flour, baking powder, baking soda, salt, and cocoa. Add the vanilla to the buttermilk. Add the cooled melted chocolate to the eggs and butter. Then alternately mix in the dry ingredients and the buttermilk.

Fill your pans about half full with batter.

Bake in the preheated oven about 40 to 45 minutes. Insert a straw or cake tester into the centers of layers. If it comes out clean (i.e., without any batter sticking to it) the cake is done and should be removed from the oven. The cakes can also be tested for doneness by pressing on them gently in the center. If they have a slightly springy feel, they are ready to come out.

MAKES TWO 10-INCH CAKE LAYERS

*We use parchment paper circles at the bottom as well. This makes our lives a lot easier (there's no danger of the bottom sticking), but is not absolutely necessary. If you do use parchment paper, we find it works best if you butter the pan, then place the circle precut to fit the pan, and butter along the edges. You can also pour into buttered cocoa dusted pans.

Lemon or Orange Cake

We use vanilla batter to make our lemon and orange cakes.

Fold 1 teaspoon of lemon or orange oil into the batter for Vanilla Cake (page 121). If you don't have easy access to such oils, use grated rind (which is where the oil comes from). The rind from about 2 pieces of fruit (either 2 lemons or 2 oranges) should sufficiently flavor your vanilla batter to turn it into lemon or orange batter. Follow directions for Cupcake Café Vanilla Cake to complete recipe.

Bohemian Walnut Cake

¾ POUND BUTTER

3 CUPS GRANULATED SUGAR

8 EGGS SEPARATED

3 CUPS PASTRY FLOUR

1 TEASPOON BAKING SODA

¼ TEASPOON SALT

1 ½ CUPS BUTTERMILK

1 ½ TEASPOONS VANILLA

1 ½ CUPS COARSELY GROUND OR
FINELY CHOPPED WALNUTS*

Thoroughly grease two 8-inch round cake pans. (For hints on no-stick pan preparation, see the Chocolate Cake recipe on page 123.) Preheat the oven to 350°F. Cream the butter and sugar together. Add the egg yolks. Sift the flour, baking powder, and salt together. Add the buttermilk to the butter, sugar, and yolk mixture, alternating with the flour mix. Beat the eggs whites till stiff but still wet. Fold into the batter and fold in the chopped walnuts.

Fill the greased 8-inch cake pans two-thirds full and bake 35–40 minutes in a 350°F oven until done. To test if cake is done, insert a straw or cake tester into the center of each layer. If it comes out clean (i.e., without any batter sticking to it), the cake is done. The cakes can also be tested for doneness by pressing on them gently in the center. If they have a slightly springy feel, they are ready to come out.

MAKES TWO 8-INCH LAYERS

*The walnuts should be chopped in a food processor or nut grinder using a few brief pulses. Another option is to chop them in a blender in three small batches taking care not to over do it and pulverize them. If you don't have access to either machine, use a rounded blade in a bowl, or a knife on a chopping board and then cover with parchment paper and crush them slightly with a rolling pin.

Carrot Cake

⅓ CUP UNBLEACHED FLOUR

½ CUP WHOLE WHEAT FLOUR

½ TEASPOON CINNAMON

⅓ TEASPOON SALT

1 TEASPOON BAKING SODA

½ CUP RAISINS

⅓ CUP TOASTED WHEAT GERM

⅔ CUP CHOPPED WALNUTS

4 EGGS

½ CUP WHITE SUGAR

½ CUP BROWN SUGAR

2⅔ CUPS GRATED CARROT*

½ CUP HONEY

2 OUNCES MELTED BUTTER

⅔ CUP OIL (SOY, CORN, OR CANOLA)

Thoroughly grease two 10-inch round cake pans. (For hints on no-stick pan preparation, see the Chocolate Cake recipe on page 123.) Preheat oven to 350°F. Sift together the unbleached flours, cinnamon, salt, and baking soda. Add the whole wheat flour and wheat germ. Combine well. Add the raisins and chopped walnut pieces. Combine well. Mix the eggs and the white and brown sugars together. Add the grated carrot, honey, oil, and melted butter. Stir well.

Fold in the flour mixture until just combined. Fill greased cake pans two-thirds full. Bake 25–30 minutes at 350°F or until done. Insert a straw or cake tester into the center of each layer. If it comes out clean (i.e., without any batter sticking to it) it is done. Cakes can also be tested for doneness by pressing on them gently in the center. If they have a slightly springy feel, they are ready to come out. Cool before frosting.

MAKES TWO 10-INCH LAYERS

*Carrots can be grated using a common cheese grater, rubbing the carrots against the medium or next-to-largest openings, or with a food processor with a grating disk.

Cupcakes

Cupcakes are made from the same batter as our layer cakes. Place cupcake papers into muffin tins and fill them slightly more than halfway. Bake at 375°F for 20 to 25 minutes. Most of our cake batters should yield somewhere between 1½ to 2½ dozen cupcakes, depending on the size of your papers and pans. Insert a straw or cake tester into the center of a cupcake—if it comes out clean (i.e., without any batter sticking to it), they're done.

After they have cooled, cupcakes can be frosted with butter cream (or another frosting) and decorated if you wish. Cupcakes make nifty vehicles for practicing a single flower. Besides the standard rose, try a large sunflower or a dahlia. Poinsettias in pink, white, or red, with a few dark green pine needles are nice. Violets also work well on cupcakes. Cupcakes decorated with the names of a child's class or teammates are popular at the Café. Use a #3 or #4 tip for writing the names. Red is probably the favorite "gender neutral" color for this. Add a tiny flower if there's room. (See Forming Flowers with Butter Cream on page 144 and subsequent recipes for specific flowers.)

Butter Cream

Unless you want to eat your cake neat—no frosting, just cake—you'll need to prepare butter cream to frost (or baste) the outside of the cake and between the layers. (A good jam is nice between the layers, too.) The butter cream you use to baste your cake is the same stuff you'll use later for writing on the cake—and decorating it, if you choose to go the whole way.

Butter cream does not take very long to put together, but the syrup you make must cool adequately before it is added to the butter, so consider making it a few hours (anywhere from 2 to 12 hours) before you plan to do your frosting. Also, remember to set out the butter to temper (that is, come to room temperature) if you will not be assisted by a microwave. Your eggs should also be room temperature (uncracked in the shell).

MAKING BUTTER CREAM

Equipment you will need:

- a saucepan or pot (at least 2-quart size) with a not-too-thin bottom, and a close-fitting lid
- a stove top
- an electric mixer (almost essential; second best is a blender and a food processor— you'd need both) or amazing strength, the patience of Job, and a heavy whisk

Optional but very handy

- a candy thermometer
- access to a microwave

Vanilla Butter Cream

4 CUPS GRANULATED SUGAR

1 CUP WATER

6 EGGS, AT ROOM TEMPERATURE

2½ POUNDS UNSALTED BUTTER,
AT ROOM TEMPERATURE

1 TEASPOON PURE VANILLA EXTRACT

To make the sugar syrup, combine the 4 cups of sugar and 1 cup water in a 2- or 3-quart saucepan and heat over medium-high (moderate) heat, stirring occasionally, until it starts to boil. When the mixture boils, put the lid on the pot for a few minutes. Cover now and again to wash the sugar crystals back into the syrup. This is particularly important for decorating purposes so that you do not end up with pieces of sugar clogging your decorating tubes.

Allow the syrup to reach 236°F, using a candy thermometer to determine this. If you do not have a thermometer, you can test the temperature by letting some of the syrup drop off the spoon back into the syrup. It should fall a bit slowly, the drops coming together to form one drop that should lengthen and just begin to form a thread; do not cook longer. If the syrup gets too hot, it will go from the "soft ball" stage to what's called "hard ball" or "hard-crack" stage. This term means that the syrup is on its way to being usable for making hard candy, and when cooled it will become brittle.

If this happens, when you add the syrup to the eggs they will not combine smoothly and instead will form an unusable mixture of sweetened eggs and bits of hard candy. You don't want this to happen, so stop heating when the syrup is at 236°F.

When your syrup is at a perfect soft ball stage, remove it from the heat and cover it. Have your eggs ready in a bowl large enough for the eggs and syrup. Beat the eggs first and then slowly add the hot sugar syrup, using an electric mixer. If you do not have an electric mixer, beat the eggs first in a blender and then gradually add the syrup to the eggs, blending continually. The syrup must be added slowly so as to gradually heat the eggs, avoiding the unpleasantness of chewy bits of candied scrambled egg in your frosting.

The egg and sugar syrup mixture, the "goo," has to cool to room temperature before it is added to the butter. Just allow it to cool in or out of the fridge. The mixture can get a sugar crust on top if it is not covered, so, if you won't be using your frosting right away, you might cover it with plastic wrap or a bowl lid. You can make the egg and sugar syrup well ahead; covered and refrigerated it will keep for several days. Let it warm awhile if it is very cold before you use it.

If you need the mixture cooled quickly, you can hasten the process by putting the mixture in a (preferably) metal bowl and setting this bowl over another larger one filled with ice cubes. Stir occasionally until it has cooled to room temperature.

When the "goo" (the egg and sugar mixture) is cool and you are ready to make butter cream, place the tempered—room temperature—butter into a mixing bowl large enough for everything. Beat the butter with an electric mixer first until it is quite smooth, then gradually add the "goo" until it is completely absorbed. This can take anywhere from 2 to 6 minutes.

For frosting or basting the cake, the butter cream can be quite soft and somewhat airy; for decorating you'll probably want it a bit firmer. Beating the butter cream longer will usually make it whiter and fluffier.

Add the vanilla after you've added the egg mix or at the same time. If the egg and sugar mixture has been stored overnight, sugar crystals will sometimes form. Use a strainer or sieve to strain the mixture and remove anything that might clog your decorating tips before you beat it into the butter.

MAKES ABOUT 10 CUPS (ENOUGH TO DECORATE ONE LARGE TWO-LAYER CAKE)

HAZARDS TO BUTTER CREAM

HUMIDITY:

Humidity can adversely affect butter cream; so can barometric pressure (changing weather conditions). After butter cream is almost mixed together it will sometimes separate somewhat, looking "cracked" and not smooth at all.

WHAT TO DO WITH "CRACKED" BUTTER CREAM:

If the butter cream separates a bit after it has been well beaten, try melting about 1 or 2 cups of it in a microwave (or slowly over hot water) and adding it back into the cracked butter cream, beating until the butter cream comes together again.

BAROMETRIC CHANGES:

On "bad butter cream days," when the weather is not clear, butter cream may tend to be less stable and is more likely to separate a bit. To avoid this, you should pay careful attention to the following:

- Take particular care to see that everything is the correct temperature. Butter that is too cold or too warm, syrup that hasn't cooled enough or that is too cold from being stored in a refrigerator, can cause the cream to separate or not combine properly in the first place.

- Mix everything carefully. Be patient, when it is ready it is ready. Sometimes it will just require longer beating. Don't be upset if at some point it looks more like soup than butter cream. Eventually, it will pull itself together and be fine.

Flavored Butter Cream

We use Vanilla Butter Cream (page 133) as a base for all of our flavored frostings. In each case add to about half a batch of butter cream:

LEMON OR ORANGE BUTTER CREAM

Butter cream can be flavored easily by adding citrus oils to the mixed Vanilla Butter Cream (page 133). Be cautious—add $\frac{1}{4}$ to $\frac{1}{2}$ teaspoon and taste it, then add just a bit more if you feel it needs it. Grated lemon or orange rind (the rind from one piece of fruit should be plenty) can be added instead of oil for frosting a cake, but not for decorating as the rind will clog the tips.

LIQUEURS

Add to Vanilla Butter Cream (page 133) 1 to 3 tablespoons liqueur to taste. Grand Marnier is a popular flavor, we've found.

CHOCOLATE BUTTER CREAM

Melt 4 to 6 ounces of unsweetened chocolate either in a double boiler or in the microwave, being careful not to burn it. Allow the chocolate to cool, then beat it into the Vanilla Butter Cream (page 133).

MOCHA BUTTER CREAM

Dissolve 2 to 3 tablespoons of strong espresso-grade instant coffee in 3 tablespoons of brewed coffee (or water) and add 2 ounces of cooled melted chocolate. Add this to Vanilla Butter Cream (page 133).

Cake Decorating

EQUIPMENT FOR FROSTING AND DECORATING

What you will need for frosting and decorating cakes:

- A spatula with a blade about 8 inches long by 1½ inches wide.

- A heavy metal (not plastic) cake stand or decorating wheel—such as a #610 by Ateco— is very useful, particularly for frosting and decorating cakes 10 inches and up.

- A piece of stiff corrugated cardboard, or Masonite, the same dimension as the bottom layer of the cake you are decorating, makes it possible to manipulate the cake independent of a cumbersome plate.

- A second cake circle or board 2 inches larger than the cake is useful for handling the cake and should help you avoid inadvertently sticking your fingers into the sides while moving the cake around to decorate it. If the cake is going to be served where it is being decorated, a regular plate (again one that has a diameter a couple of inches larger than your cake) can be used instead.

- Several 10-inch plastic-coated fabric decorating bags. We use Ateco's #3110. One dozen will probably do, 2 dozen would be luxurious. Be careful washing them. Use hot water, no soap, and let them air-dry at room temperature. Don't use the microwave.

- One to two dozen plastic couplings for the pastry bags.

- An assortment of tips.

> #3 (plain point for writing).
>
> #103 (rose).
>
> #104 (rose).
>
> #59 (a small curved petal).
>
> #352 (leaf).

Tips you may want to add later:

> #2 (a smaller point).
>
> #4, #5 (a larger point).
>
> #60, #61 (a larger small curved petal).
>
> #16 (a star tip for borders such as shells).
>
> #20 (for larger borders).
>
> #67 or #68 (a different leaf tip, particularly favored for poinsettias at Christmastime at the Café).
>
> #45 (for a smaller and larger ribbon, although called a "carnation" tip).
>
> #81 a tip with a small semicircular opening, for small lilac petals and lily of the valley.

There are many other tips you might care to experiment with, although I won't be referring to them in this book.

- Commercial quality food dye or coloring, such as Chefmaster Liquid paste. (I've used their color names, but some other brands use them, too.)

Most vital colors to have:

> lemon yellow
> royal red
> bright purple
> royal blue
> black

egg yellow or "egg shade"

tulip red

"bright pink"

"baker's rose"

fuchsia

bright blue

Less important but nice to have

orange or "bright orange"

burgundy

violet

brown

- Cups, to mix colored frosting in. We use 10-ounce paper cups, but coffee mugs or small bowls would do as well, or plastic jars available in some art shops.
- Long iced tea spoons are more comfortable for mixing up colored frosting than regular teaspoons, but regular teaspoons or forks will do.

BASTING OR FROSTING CAKES

We do wedding cakes and sheet cakes and, under some duress, will cut cake into shapes, but most of what we do are round layer cakes filled and frosted with butter cream, and this is what I describe here.

First of all, no matter what shape your cake is, or how you plan to decorate it, or even if you wish to decorate it at all, a cake ready to be frosted in butter cream must be cool or the frosting will melt.

With large cakes this means you need to be sure the centers of the layers aren't warm. If they are, the layers can slide apart when assembled.

Frosting a cake can be a big deal or not, depending on your aesthetic outlook and how picky you are. Straight, even, perpendicular sides as smooth as possible and a level, flat, smooth top are not essential for most decorating, the only exception being (stacked, multitiered) wedding cakes.

We will proceed, though, under the assumption that this symmetrical crisp cylinder is our ideal.

For frosting purposes you will probably want your butter cream a bit warmer than for decorating. If it feels too stiff, a few seconds of microwaving should help.

If you are trying to create a smooth surface and hide a few cake crumbs it seems to be expeditious to frost the cake twice.

First place the bottom layer on your "cake cardboard" (that's the corrugated circle or rectangle that is the same size as your bottom layer).

Spread over the top whatever you are using to fill the cake between the layers (such as butter cream, either the same or a different flavor from the outside, or jam).

If you are using jam or preserves, stop ½ to 1 inch short of the outside edge so it can be sealed with butter cream and won't leak.

Cover that layer with the top layer of cake. If your layers are not level, you can rectify the situation somewhat now. Make certain to place the lower or thinner sides at opposite ends so that the thicker or higher part of one layer will meet and rest against the thinner or lower part of the other.

Extra frosting can also be used to bolster up an edge. If only one layer is uneven or exceedingly rounded, you can level it, using a serrated knife to remove the offending protuberance. On most cakes though, I wouldn't bother to expunge a rounded top.

When you are more or less satisfied with your would-be cylinder, frost the sides of the cake using a minimal amount of frosting just to seal the cake. See to it that the top layer is directly over the bottom layer so that the sides are straight from top to bottom. Use the whole flat side of the spatula rather than just the short end, and do not be afraid to use some pressure. Don't be concerned if the crumbs still show.

Frost the top lightly again and allow it to chill in the refrigerator.

When cooled, the crumbs will be sealed off, and you can frost with more butter cream as

desired. Again, use most of the length of the spatula to do this, using broad strokes with some pressure. When your cake looks smooth enough to suit you, place the first cake cardboard with the cake onto another, larger board (your second cake circle or board 2 inches larger than the cake) and glue the boards together with some butter cream; if you prefer (and will be serving the cake where it will be decorated) you can place your cake on a cake plate. Refrigerate until needed.

INSCRIBING A FLOWERED CAKE

If a cake is going to be decorated with butter cream flowers and it is going to be inscribed, the inscription should be done next after the cake has chilled. Chilling will give you a more solid writing surface.

It is better to put an inscription on a cake before the other decoration for several reasons. It is obviously easier to place the inscription pleasingly and fit everything on without having to scrunch any of the words. Also, if for any reason you wish to change it, it can be easily removed and done again until you are pleased with the result. After your writing is encircled with flowers it is difficult to remove or change it without gouging the cake or smashing the flowers.

If writing on cakes is new to you, you can practice first on any washable surface, such as a cake stand or countertop.

Make up a pastry bag, inserting the large piece of the plastic coupler into the bag first and securing a #3 tip over the bag to the couple with the ring part, both on the outside of the bag.

Mix up an appropriate color or just beat up some plain Vanilla Butter Cream (page 133) in a cup if you are practicing. Place the butter cream into the pastry bag. Use enough so the bag feels comfortable to handle even if your inscription will use only a tablespoon or two, probably about 5 to 8 ounces liquid measure. What you don't use up writing can be recycled for decorating later.

There are people who can write on cakes beautifully straight off with almost no practice at all. For those people, rules as to color and placement may be freely broken. Most important is to learn to trust and like your own handwriting. Practice by all means, but do it so you feel comfortable writing, not so your writing looks like someone else's. The less tortured and more spontaneous your writing, the more likely it will look pleasing to the eye. I have listed some other advice but none that can really compensate for writing that looks slow, tentative, and uncomfortable with itself.

Choosing an appropriate color can improve the effect of very good to mediocre writing and soften the blow of writing with a still-not-comfortable hand.

If writing on cakes is not your strongest suit, don't do it in colors that will grab attention away from the rest of your decoration. Avoid using colors that are very dark or very bright. Try paler shades, subtle versions of a color that you are planning to use in the decoration or one that will complement those colors.

The occasion is often the deciding factor in choosing the color of the inscription. If a cake is meant to be very elegant, it might be a good idea to use an inscription that all but disappears, such as a very pale blue to silver, sage, gold, or rose. For a birthday, most spontaneous-looking scripts need not disappear into the cake. One might choose a fresher, more definite color. Still, look for one that won't detract from your decoration.

Using the right size tip (#2, #3, #4, or #5) for the way you write and the size of the cake is important as well. A good rule is to use a #2 or #3 to write on a 6-inch cake; a #3 for an 8-inch cake; a #3 or #4 for a 10-inch; #4 for a 12-inch or 14-inch cake. (If you are not pleased with your writing, try a different-size tip.)

If your writing looks too hesitant, perhaps a #2 or #3 is too slow for you, forcing you to use too much pressure and write too slowly. If your writing looks too heavy, try using a smaller tip, such as a #3 instead of a #4, leaving a #4 only for larger cakes.

Unlike when you write on paper, you will be maintaining only a slight contact with the cake surface. Most of us find it helpful to support the hand holding the bag with our other hand, either under our writing hand or under the bag, to keep from feeling as though we are attempting to write in the air.

FORMING FLOWERS WITH BUTTER CREAM

Forming Roses

While a rose is not the easiest flower to make, it is, I think, a good one to start with. It is a flower most people will want to be able to make and, once having mastered the necessary dexterity with a pastry bag to do a rose, all other flowers should come rather easily.

After you have read through this section and are ready to practice making flowers, make a batch of butter cream. If you are not going to decorate something to be eaten, your practice butter cream can be scooped up and reused again and again for practice purposes. (Think Play-Doh.)

When you are first practicing a flower shape, start off using butter cream with very little if any food coloring. The more dye you add to your butter cream, the less stable it will become—that is, the more likely it is to break down into its component parts.

Begin by scooping out 6 to 8 ounces (liquid measure) of butter cream from your batch and placing it in a 10-ounce or larger cup or bowl. Immediately before filling your pastry bag, beat or stir the butter cream with a spoon or fork. The texture should be smooth and heavy. Now is the time to beat it a bit more if the texture isn't just right. If your butter cream doesn't look or feel "right" refer to the section Hazards to Butter Cream on page 135.

A good surface to practice on is your decorating wheel. (Refer to the section on Equipment [page 137] if you're not familiar with decorating wheels.) A plastic cutting board, or

even a wooden one, is also good. If you want to use wax paper, make sure it is weighted down, or "glue" it down with some butter cream, so that it doesn't stick to the butter cream coming from your decorating bag and lift up while you're working.

Make up a pastry bag: put the plastic cone-shaped coupler on the inside of the bag with the smaller end of the coupler pushed as far as it will go into the smaller end of the pastry bag. Place a #103 tip over the small end of the bag and secure it with the ring part of the coupler placed over the tip of the bag and screwed on tight. A #104 tip makes a larger rose, but I suggest you practice with the #103 first. Now you are

ready to fill your bag (about a half to two-thirds full) with butter cream. Eventually you'll know just how much is comfortable for you.

Twist the extra fabric gathered at the end of the bag to keep it closed. Hold the bag so that the short base of the rose tip is against your practice surface (or "the cake") and the long sides are almost

vertical or flange out at an obtuse angle. Start by practicing how to make petals by pressing out frosting ¾ inch to one inch at a time in random formation. Attempt to make these butter cream petals stand vertically at an obtuse angle from your surface. Practice starting and stopping to get a sense of control over how the butter cream flows out of the bag and how much pressure you need.

To make your rose, start by squeezing out a base for the flower. A base of butter cream can be piped a couple of different ways and since your base won't show when you are done, you can do it any way that proves most comfortable for you. Use your #103 tip and pipe to make a round base about ¾ inch in diameter. I prefer the circular shape. Onto this, pipe a circle, an "O" or two overlapping "U"s. This will be your rose center. A small one is fine, an open one suggests a more fully opened flower. Start adding petals around it, a little larger and at a more open obtuse angle as you go. Some can fold out over themselves near or at the perimeter if you like. Studying the color photographs should help. You can turn your decorating wheel to work your way around the base if you like, or just move your bag with your hand and wrist.

(If you're trying to make a flat rose against the side of a cake or a small rose or rosebud you would skip the base-making step.)

Doing this over and over is the only trick to learning it. Once you have the hang of it, it will quickly become second nature. Until then, just persevere. "Just how long should this take?" the easily discouraged might now be asking. Having taught a number of decorators, I can say definitively—it depends. Some people pick this up quickly, while for others it may seem to take forever. On the other hand, I've noticed that some of the slower starters will eventually make the nicest cakes with the best and most interesting roses. So, slow starters, take heart.

The best source for inspiration as to coloring, shape, and size is probably to look at real rosebushes. Vary the size of your roses. Think of a rosebush in a garden, with all different-sized roses on one bush at different stages of bloom, more or less open, and turned in different ways. Group roses together by color, but try to use a deeper shade and a lighter shade of the same color together.

Try to avoid covering your cake with identical-looking flowers that suggest they just came out of a florist's refrigerator.

Using two shades of the same color, a darker one and a lighter one in the same bag, is a good idea. Also a warmer, earthy color combined with cooler colors can be quite effective.

Making Colored Butter Cream for Roses

WHITE

No dye, just well-beaten Vanilla Butter Cream (page 133). If your natural-colored frosting is not as white as you'd like, rebeating will change a yellowish-cream color to a whiter shade.

Roses in white go well with any color, but particularly with flowers in the yellow, blue, and purple spectrum. Yellow or yellow-green centers work well to set off white roses, as do dark leaves with a bit of red in them. Use white flowers to cool off a composition that has a lot of orange or coral.

PINK

For a dark pink, use enough red dye added to Vanilla Butter Cream (page 133) so it is not yet red. For a more pastel shade, closer to white, it is often easier to mix up a darker one and use a little of that color to tint another cup of white butter cream.

Pink roses go particularly well with other shades of pink, coral, light red, and rose. The purple family is also a successful match, particularly if the flowers include those deep shades with a lot of pink in them. Be careful when using pink with yellow that the result is not too saccharine. Blue and pink—often requested by our customers for baby shower cakes— benefit from adding touches of purple, even small amounts, as well as other "bridge" colors, such as mauve and lavender. White can cool off a too-pink cake that you wish to keep essentially pink. More dye will, of course, produce a darker color.

A COOL PINK

Add to 8 ounces Vanilla Butter Cream (page 133):

3 to 4 drops royal red
1 to 2 drops baker's rose, hot pink, or deep or bright pink

A WARMER PINK (LIGHT)

Add to 8 ounces Vanilla Butter Cream (page 133):

2 to 5 drops tulip red royal
2 drops royal red

ROSE

Rose is really a dusty deep pink, with purple and a bit of red mixed in. It is a lovely bridge color between cool and warm tones. Its earthy neutrality can calm things down a bit, keep a cake from being too childish or too saccharine, and can add solidity to a predominantly pastel cake without being jarring.

Add to 8 ounces Vanilla Butter Cream (page 133):

10 drops tulip red
3 drops royal red or red red
3 drops bright purple

This produces a light rose.

FOR A DARKER SHADE ADD

3 more drops bright purple (making it 6 in all).

FOR A STILL DARKER ROSE

Increase to a total of 8 drops bright purple and 8 drops royal red per 10 drops tulip red.

By using colors you've already mixed, for instance a cup of pink, you can make a good rose color that is nicely related to what you have used already.

PEACH

Peach is to orange as pink is to red. Kind of. Peach is that color that really doesn't go with blue. People ordering wedding cakes love to ask for "peach, but no pink," "coral, but no orange" and "salmon, but no pink and no orange." You cross your fingers (just try decorating with your fingers crossed) and hope the pastel shade you've mixed up stays that pastel shade you've mixed up, and doesn't change into something darker, or redder, or yellower. Shades of butter cream with yellow dye can darken after they are chilled, the yellow becoming more pronounced. Horrors!

Peach does go well with white and champagne and all those other mysterious off-whites. It does well with yellows (particularly pale ones), coral, salmon, orange, light reds to dark burgundy, and pink. As I've said, I've got no use for it with blue, but that's just me. If you do use purple or lavender with peach, try to use some pink as well, and remember white.

Add to 8 ounces Vanilla Butter Cream (page 133):

Formula #1

1 to 2 drops royal red
2 drops tulip red
2 drops lemon yellow

Formula #2

1 to 2 drops tulip red
2 to 4 drops egg shade

Formula #3

1 to 3 drops bright orange
1 to 2 drops egg shade

CORAL OR SALMON

Coral or salmon, darker than peach but not really orange, makes a nice intermediate color on a cake with pastels and/or primary colors. Like rose, it should not be too pure or too muddy. The colorings suggested are just approximate. You'll have to watch what you are doing and adjust the dye accordingly.

Add to 8 ounces Vanilla Butter Cream (page 133)

Formula #1

3 to 5 drops tulip red
4 to 6 drops lemon yellow
3 to 5 drops royal red
1 drop bright purple (optional)

Formula #2
4 to 6 drops red red
3 to 6 drops egg yellow
2 to 4 drops burgundy

WARNING: Pastel colors sometimes darken as they warm and some pink shades seem to darken as they chill. You may want to go lighter when mixing pale peach to medium coral shades.

REDS

One of the fun things about using professional food coloring is being able to mix up a good satisfying red. Those who have never before experienced real red dye may have a tendency to overdo it the first time and use too much dye. You will probably find you need far less than you realize. Red is a color that will often darken after it has been mixed. Try to get more mileage out of the coloring you do use, by using it intelligently.

Placed next to lighter shades, a medium dark red can look quite lush and rich enough without being saturated with food dye. A lighter red used with a stronger one will take on the good characteristics of the deeper shade, and keep a strong color from looking dead. For roses, I think reds that are really a mix of shades work best. Red roses go well with other red roses—particularly when there are many shades of red. The leaves on such a cake are important, greens with purple or red in them integrate nicely, as do reddish stems with some blue in them. Pinks, purples, and oranges, including mauves and lavenders, roses and corals, go well with reds. Red can be a good choice to use with blue flowers, because it is not overwhelmed, as some colors can be. Some white or pink used with the reds and blues would be a good idea. Red and yellow are a more difficult combination. I like red and yellow combined in the same flower, as in a tulip or dahlia, but yellow and red roses need a lot of other stuff happening to work.

Peace roses (a variegated hybrid rose that is usually a pale yellow blushing to a peach or coral shade toward the top of the petals) are possible with red roses. Of course, all this is highly subjective.

Add to 8 ounces Vanilla Butter Cream (page 133):

A LIGHTER WARM RED

8 to 12 drops tulip red
8 to 12 drops red red

A COOLER DARK RED

8 to 16 drops royal red
4 to 8 drops bright purple
6 to 12 drops red red

BURGUNDY

15 to 20 drops burgundy
10 to 15 drops red red

A LIGHTER COOL RED

5 to 6 drops red
7 to 9 drops royal red
5 to 7 drops bright pink

YELLOW

When mixing up yellow butter cream for roses, go easy on the yellow dye. The petals will reflect yellow onto one another and appear to be a stronger color. Much of the time the butter cream will be slightly yellow to begin with. Try not to mix too flat a color. You can't be too subtle when trying for a variation in tone here, or it won't show at all given yellow's bright reflective quality. Try making roses with an egg shade butter cream and a light lemon yellow mixed up separately and put through the same bag.

Add to 8 ounces Vanilla Butter Cream (page 133):

> 4 to 6 drops egg shade
> 1 to 2 drops tulip red
> Put in the same bag with:
> 8 ounces Vanilla Butter Cream (page 133)
> 1 to 2 drops egg shade
> 2 drops lemon yellow

Dilute further with white butter cream as you go, using the same bag. Yellow roses are good with variegated ones such as peach and yellow Peace roses, corals, white, off-whites, blue, and purple flowers.

VARIEGATED PEACE ROSES

To create these variegated hybrids you start off with a darker yellow base or center, then pipe petals around the center using:

1. a pale yellow (1 to 2 drops lemon yellow)

2. a tablespoon or so of plain Vanilla Butter Cream (page 133)

3. a peach shade (2 drops lemon yellow or 3 drops tulip red), added to 8 ounces Vanilla Butter Cream (page 133).

Arrange these three shades in your bag so that the yellow is on one side of the short base of the tip, (or bottom of the bag), the plain Vanilla Butter Cream is in the middle, and the peach color is next to it, so that it will be piped through at the top. Use a #103 or #104 rose tip.

CHAMPAGNE

Champagne is a color closer to yellow than pink, but closest to white. I suggest using yellow or yellow-green in the center and varying the strength of your color throughout the flower. Try to put lighter petals toward the outside of the rose by adding more plain Vanilla Butter Cream (page 133) to the pastry bag as you go.

Add to 8 ounces Vanilla Butter Cream (page 133):

   1 to 2 drops egg shade
   1 drop tulip red

Or better still, add a little mixed yellow and a little mixed peach to a cup of white.

OFF-WHITES

A variety of good off-whites can be mixed for roses using a cup of plain Vanilla Butter Cream (page 133) and just a tablespoon or less of another color you've already mixed up. Green, lavender, ocher, and orange shades can make very nice off-white shades for flowers.

LAVENDER

Lavender mixed up for roses should be a very pastel shade of purple.

Add to 8 ounces Vanilla Butter Cream (page 133):

   1 to 3 drops purple or violet

Lavender's slightly gray or silvery quality can be used to add something rather cool and elegant to a composition. Pale lavender roses in less pink shades can create a staid, unexpected look.

MAUVE

Mauve is related to lavender and rose, and can have lavender's elegant qualities as well. It can, however, be an elusive shade and takes a bit of practice to mix up. It can be a warm color used with purples, blues, and whites, or a cool one used with red, rust, coral, peach, and some pinks. While it is one of the trickiest colors to keep from becoming too muddy or too heavy, it is worth the effort. Just take your time.

Add to 8 ounces Vanilla Butter Cream (page 133):

3 to 6 drops purple
4 to 8 drops tulip red
3 to 6 drops bright violet
2 to 4 drops red red

With both mauve and lavender flowers, yellow and yellow with green centers provide a contrast that is like a sneaky citrusy tang, not too obvious but not boring either.

LEAVES FOR ROSES AND GENERAL COMMENTS ON THE USE OF LEAVES

With your roses you will need leaves. I write "need" because I have discovered that many people think they do not *want* leaves. I don't know why, but some people are quite certain they don't want green on their cakes at all. Any leaf, even one that is pale and not really very green, will make a butter cream flower look more like a flower. Leaves can also help clarify for everyone else what kind of flower you've made. Green isn't really the issue. A chocolate leaf can work wonders for a chocolate rose.

Often perfectly nice flowers on a cake will look meager because not enough care was taken with the leaves. Don't give them short shrift! You need not cover your cake with leaves. Unless you're trying to produce a jungle, a few good leaves will suffice.

As for leaf *color*, the right color can be anything from a pale silver that is less green than sage, to a deep mahogany brown. What makes a leaf color right is what it does for the flower it sets off. What does it do for the mood of a composition? Aesthetic sensibilities vary like crazy so you might not agree if I stated flat out that a particular green is elegant, or cheerful, or youthful. Even if I used the same color roses, I might use a different leaf color for an engagement cake than a fiftieth-birthday cake, and yet another leaf color on a cake for an eight-year-old.

I like earthy greens that include some of the flower colors in them. They can provide contrasting cool and warm tones, and at the same time relate to the flower colors directly. Take time to look at leaves in nature if possible, or landscape paintings, if nature isn't providing appropriate examples at the moment. Leaves are shadow and light. They can make a cake seem to breathe and a flower to be growing. If what you are trying for is a cake that resembles a garden, you'll need to be that much more serious about your leaves.

Consider scale when you do your leaves. Very small leaves will be fine with tiny flowers, but a heavy flower needs a bigger leaf. Try to think of what is appropriate for that flower. For instance, a tulip leaf that looks reasonably enough like a tulip leaf will suggest that the flower you have made is a tulip rather than a crocus, even when the flower itself is indistinguishable. Or when you've mixed and piped that perfect peony leaf or two next to your peony, and it's just the right size for your flower, everyone will know that it is a peony, and not some klutzy attempt at a rose. (By the same token a "rose" surrounded by carrots and peas, will be seen as a cabbage.)

Too many blossoms jammed together with no leaves will look more like a funeral wreath than either a garden or a bouquet. Give your flowers room, use leaves to space them out. You can use leaves to anchor thin, flighty, and pastel-colored flowers or, alternatively, to provide a little calm on cakes with bright vibrant flowers.

LEAVES FOR ROSES

Try to mix two greens when making leaves, one more shadowy and one with a lighter quality. Put them together in one pastry bag with a #352 tip, half to one side and half to the other. Imitating roughly the shapes given, try for leaves from half as long as your rose is wide, up to as long or even a touch longer than your rose is wide. Two of the many possible color combinations are given here:

Add to 6 ounces Vanilla Butter Cream (page 133):

LEAF FORMULA #1:

   2 to 6 drops royal blue
   2 to 4 drops egg shade
   2 to 4 drops lemon yellow

Add half of this to 4 ounces Vanilla Butter Cream (page 133). This will be the lighter green. To the rest of the first green add 2 ounces of Vanilla Butter Cream and *one* of the following:

1 to 3 drops purple or
1 to 2 drops burgundy or
2 to 5 drops egg shade or
1 to 2 drops bright purple

This will be the darker green.

LEAF FORMULA #2:

Add to 6 ounces Vanilla Butter Cream (page 133):

4 to 5 drops lemon yellow
4 drops violet
2 to 3 drops bright blue

STEMS FOR ROSES AND GENERAL COMMENTS ON THE USE OF STEMS

Stems may be used with roses and other flowers, as can light branches, to introduce a linear element to the composition. They make a nice break from all those solid forms. Any leaf color — from green to reddish brown — can be used, as can a mixture of two colors. For stems, use any tip between a #3 and a #6, the larger tips for heavier stems or branches. A few thorns can be added, as well, using the same color and tip.

Forming Peonies

An open peony is done like an exploding rose. Use a #103 tip and almost any of the rose colors, excluding shades of coral and orange and leaning toward bluer shades of red and pink. Fashion them the way you would a rose, but with many more petals, and with the petals not quite as wide and slightly longer.

Peonies that are not yet open are ball-shaped. Use the same #103 or a #61 tip and wrap the petals around each other to make a sphere that may or may not open out slightly.

The leaves of a peony are dark, glossy, and sometimes shot with red. Using a pastry bag with a #352 tip attached, add some burgundy to a deep forest green. The leaf is longer than a rose leaf and will form an almost fan-like configuration that, located near your peony flower, will tell everyone you are indeed trying to make a peony, not an exploded rose.

OTHER FLOWERS
FLOWERS WITH PETALS THAT RADIATE FROM THE CENTER

Forming Daisies

Daisies are actually much easier to do than roses. Many flowers can be made using the same tips and more or less the same technique. We'll start off making white daisies with yellow centers.

You'll need to make up three pastry bags, two #4's and one #59. The bag with the #59 tip will be your white pastry bag. Just mix your butter cream until it feels heavy and smooth and as close to "white" as you can get it. Fill the bag two-thirds full. The two #4 bags will be filled with two different yellows as follows:

To make a warm orangy yellow: add to about 6 ounces Vanilla Butter Cream (page 133):

2 to 3 drops lemon yellow
4 to 5 drops egg shade
1 to 2 drops tulip red

In a second bag:
Add to 6 ounces Vanilla Butter Cream (page 133):

4 drops lemon yellow
2 drops egg shade
2 drops royal blue or bright blue

This will be your greener yellow.

First practice making daisy petals randomly, trying for an even stroke slightly tapered at the end, or a lengthened petal approaching an ellipse, adding a little more pressure toward the middle. Then practice arranging them radiating from a center circle about ½ to ¾ inch in diameter. First use the greener yellow around the edge of this circle making many small dots with the first #4 bag and some in the very center.

Fill in the rest of the center with the more orange yellow, also making small dots or points with your second #4 bag.

You may find it helpful to turn your decorating wheel as you form these flowers. A lightly-petaled daisy-type flower should have about a minimum of seven petals. A more densely petaled daisy might have twelve to sixteen or more overlapping petals.

There are many daisies and daisy-like flowers that can be done this way. You don't need to use just these yellows for centers; there are many shades—from a pale green, through yellow, to a raw sienna or slightly "dirty" looking (or toned down) orange—that would do nicely. Some other flowers and their petal colors are:

ENGLISH DAISY
white or light rose petals

MICHAELMAS DAISY
very pale (royal) blue petals

SHASTA DAISY
fuchsia

BLACK-EYED SUSAN

orangy-yellow petals, use black or black-brown for the centers

LEAVES FOR DAISIES

I prefer to borrow a leaf from a cultivated relative of the daisy, rather than try to do wild daisy foliage on a cake. The wild daisy leaf is complicated and tends to look contrived and over-worked in butter cream. Instead, I recommend a simpler leaf, or, if a cake will have just daisies for decoration, try doing a background before you do the flowers, in leaf green, suggesting daisy foliage, without trying to be too literal. Use a #350 tip and keep it light and as flat against the cake as you can.

Daisies are relatively easy to fashion on the vertical side of a cake. If gravity presents a problem, dig in slightly with your pastry bag as you pipe the petals.

Forming Sunflowers

Although sunflowers come in many color combinations, the instructions here are for yellow sunflowers with dark centers. It is best to mix more than one yellow to work with from the start. Sunflowers will look much better if there is some variation in the petal color. Yellow is a very strong color, and too much of any one shade is definitely too much. If it helps, imagine your sunflower out-of-doors, with sunlight passing through part of the flower and perhaps half of it shaded by itself.

Here are two formulas for yellow petals (just to start you off):

Add in all cases to 8 ounces Vanilla Butter Cream (page 133):

Formula #1:

6 to 10 drops egg shade
10 to 18 drops lemon yellow

Formula #2:

10 to 15 drops egg shade
2 to 4 drops purple
4 to 5 drops lemon yellow

Make up a bag with a #352 tip attached to it. Fill the bag, alternating colors about a tablespoon at a time. Alternatively, put your two colors into the bag side by side.

Practice petals radiating from the circumference of an imaginary circle. (Your center should be about 2 inches.) Make the petals about one inch long. While the petals should radiate out from your circle, try turning the bag a bit as you go, so each one lies a bit differently from the one next to it, giving the sunflower a lively, even powerful feel. You should find a happy satisfaction doing sunflowers. They do not pose technical bugaboos. There is an immediacy not unlike drawing with pastels, with the same graphic quality. They can be quite expressive and still look like sunflowers.

Not all sunflowers have dark centers, but I prefer to use rich strong colors, equal in strength to the petal color. These centers will be black and dark reddish brown.

SUNFLOWER CENTERS

Add to 8 ounces Vanilla Butter Cream (page 133):

BLACK

A couple short squirts black dye (10 to 15 drops)
A few drops brown or burgundy

DARK REDDISH BROWN

Formula #1:

8 to 14 drops brown
4 to 6 drops tulip red

Formula #2:

8 to 12 drops purple
6 to 12 drops egg shade
3 to 5 drops red red

Make up a pastry bag with #350 or #352 tip. Alternately fill your bag with two colors such as the black and a brown, about 2 to 4 tablespoons each, until it is half to two-thirds full. Alternatively, you can instead make up two bags, filling one with brown and the other with black. Pipe small seedlike points around and around the inside of your sunflower, filling the whole center circle with black and brown "seeds."

LEAVES FOR SUNFLOWERS

The leaves for sunflowers can be rather large. Use the #352 tip again. Just pipe them slowly to make a large leaf or go over one of the edges again to extend it a bit. When mixing your leaf color, try for a green that is cool and not too bright. Here is one formula:

Add to 8 ounces Vanilla Butter Cream (page 133):

2 to 5 drops royal blue
3 to 4 drops egg shade
2 to 4 drops lemon yellow
3 to 4 drops purple

Another sunflower variation is:

Add some more butter cream to your leftover yellow color and then a bit of blue (3 to 4 drops) and a bit of your center black color. Particularly on a cake decorated with sunflowers alone (which are pretty popular at present), the stems or stalks can be made using the same bags as for your leaves. Add some more plain Vanilla Butter Cream (page 133) to mix a paler green, or mix your pale green first to make stems, deepening it afterward for your leaves. Use the #352 or #350 tip and draw stalks onto your cake going over them a couple of times, letting them terminate at your flowers. I think it is more pleasing to let them "grow"—not strictly up and down, but on a diagonal, bending a bit, and letting them cross one another. I'd suggest you depict some of your sunflowers from angles other than straight on. Use elliptical centers turned different ways with shorter and longer petals to create an illusion of perspective. Use the sides of your cake. Sunflowers look good on the sides of cakes, and are not difficult to do. Use the sides for stems, too.

Varying the size of your flowers adds to the illusion of distance and space. I would definitely not recommend letting the edge of your cake run through the center of a large sunflower, however, as it is likely the sunflower, half on one plane and half on another, will look like an old rug folded over the side of your cake. You can place a flower nicely over the edge of the cake just not distributed on your two planes (top and side) in a fifty/fifty fashion. Much better to place a sunflower so at least two-thirds to seven-eighths of it are on one plane and only the remaining one-eighth to one-third on the other.

For sunflowers that cover the edge, try to fashion the petals in a slightly upright direction, away from the cake and all going in roughly the same direction. Try to think of this flower as being supported on its stalk, on neither the top or vertical plane but suspended at some angle between the two.

MORE THREE-DIMENSIONAL FLOWERS
WITH PETALS RADIATING FROM THE CENTER

Forming Zinnias

Zinnias come in an assortment of pinks, oranges, reds, yellows, and white. Their colors and petals are bright and guileless. If you are trying for a decoration that's extremely cheerful, zinnias are the perfect choice.

Unlike most flowers, a zinnia petal is best done with one color well mixed before being placed in the bag. Use a #59 tip for the petals. For the center make up a yellow and place it in a bag with a #3 point attached.

A zinnia is formed by layers of petals, the number of layers vary from one or two to a snow-ball of six or more. One to three inches are normal sizes for the flowers. The centers vary, both relative to the size of the flowers, and between types of zinnias. The flowers with the most layers of petals seem to have the smallest centers (just a few dots) while some of the simpler ones have a larger open ring for a center. The centers should be just a series of dots and not too heavy, in a small patch or a slightly larger ring, less than an inch in diameter.

When fashioning zinnias, it is best to start with the bottom layer of petals and work up, adding the center last.

LEAVES—FOR ZINNIAS

Use a #352 tip to make zinnia leaves of a medium warm green. Pipe the leaves in oblong shapes approximately one-half to two-thirds as long as the flowers are wide.

Forming Dahlias

Dahlias are similar in construction to zinnias. They can also have any number of layers or rings of petals. Using a #352 tip, layer the petals the same way you would a zinnia, from the bottom ring upward. They can be from simple to ball-shaped (pompon dahlias). The centers are more solid than those of zinnias. Dahlia colors include shades of rose to red to burgundy, shades of lavender to reddish purple, yellows, oranges, and white. The colors can be quite deep, making a striking contrast to a yellow or light green center. To shape the centers, see the suggestions for making daisy centers (see page 159).

LEAVES FOR DAHLIAS

Dahlia leaves are medium green and oval-shaped. Some varieties have smooth edges; others have rough edges.

Forming Chrysanthemums

This family includes blooms that are anywhere from less than 1 inch in diameter to giant spider mums that are 6 inches around. There are varieties with single or double layers of petals, as well as some with a dozen or so layers. In nature, even the petal shape of chrysanthemums is not a constant. They can be rounded, like the zinnia, or more angular like the dahlia, or they can be thin and straight. Mums can resemble pointy sea urchins or porcupines, shaggy sea anemones or cheerleader pompons, as well as daisies. An autumn cake can be decorated with mums alone and include a variety of color, size, and texture.

The numerous petals of a mum make them easy to do. In fact it is difficult to ruin a mum; if it isn't turning out to be one kind, you can turn it into another. They can take quite a bit of over-working that other flowers with fewer petals won't. Mums come in almost all colors including blue; the autumn colors (such as burgundy, gold, rust, and orange) are particular favorites. Mums can have a center rather like the dahlia or daisy (see page 159) or one that is somewhat smaller, or none at all. Use any of the following tips for petals: #5, #350, #59.

LEAVES FOR CHRYSANTHEMUMS

A chrysanthemum leaf is variegated—like an oak leaf. Mix a dusty warm green and use a #352 tip on the piping bag. Pipe the leaf forward and then backtrack over what you have done, going forward and back three or four times.

FLOWERS FASHIONED LIKE A CUP OR VASE

Forming Tulips

When fashioning a tulip in butter cream, think of it as a small cup fashioned from 6 petals shaped like the bowl of a wineglass. Placing the petals as if they were growing in a mostly up-right direction (tulips tend to grow straight up) with longish, upright leaves will add greatly to their pose as tulips. You can mix up any of a great variety of colors for tulips. I've listed several color possibilities below. (For others see the colors listed under Making Colored Butter Cream [page 147].)

DEEP PINK

Add to 8 ounces Vanilla Butter Cream (page 133):

    2 to 3 drops royal red
    2 to 3 drops "brite" pink

TULIP RED

    8 to 15 drops tulip red

TULIP YELLOW

    4 to 7 drops lemon yellow
    3 to 5 drops egg shade

REDDISH ORANGE

    2 to 3 drops red red
    3 to 6 drops orange
    2 to 4 drops tulip red

Any two of the above choices used together will make a nice variegated tulip. Put the yellow into the bag first, distributing it all over the inside, then open the bag and add orange or red. White and red can be used in the same way. Use a #59, #60, or #61 tip to make tulips.

Purple, lavender, peach, white, burgundy, and pale and medium pinks are some other tulip colors. Variegated varieties include white and red, white and pink, yellow with red or orange with red, and red with burgundy.

First pipe three petals together to be the far side of the tulip, with the part facing you the inside. Then pipe three more over these, turning the bag so the front of these, the side facing you, will be the outside of the tulip. Some can be more open or closed; often four or even two strokes will complete the illusion of a whole closed tulip. Tulips require a subtle movement of the wrist that takes some practice.

LEAVES FOR TULIPS

Tulips are, of course, bulbs and their leaves should suggest this. Place the leaves as though originating at the earth's surface. They usually grow vertically with some curve, first out from the base, then in, and then out slightly at the end. Use a #352 to make the leaves. Here are two possible tulip leaf greens:

Add to 8 ounces of Vanilla Butter Cream (page 133):

TULIP LEAF GREEN #1:

   3 to 5 drops royal blue
   1 to 3 drops lemon yellow
   3 to 4 drops egg shade

A COOLER TULIP LEAF GREEN #2:

   2 drops purple
   2 drops "brite" blue
   3 drops lemon yellow

A tablespoon of a lavender, or pale blue, could be added to your leaf bag to give the color a slightly frosted appearance.

Forming Crocuses

Crocuses are done in a manner similar to tulips, but should be made to look as if growing low to the ground. Colors include blue and purple and gold. The leaves are thin and straight, almost like grass. If the inside of the crocus flower shows some, dots of yellow or orange could be piped on to suggest stamens.

Forming Lilies

Lilies are another flower (like tulips) that you might think of as a cup or a cone, but in the case of lilies the petals should appear to turn out, away from the center. Six petals is the usual number, but often doing five looks better. I use a #352 tip. As with a tulip, the first 3 petals form the back wall of the lily, the front of these petals will be the interior of the lily. The center petal of these 3 petals may end abruptly, as if the end of the petal is turned away from the viewer, and cannot be seen. The 2 petals on either side may turn out, or up and out, or seem to have their ends turned away and partly hidden from the viewer, too. The next 2 or 3 petals are piped over the first 3 petals and should finish with their ends turned out toward the viewer. The different varieties of lilies are made using the appropriately colored butter creams—which means, of course, that for white lilies you'll mix up white butter cream. Adding the corresponding anthers makes your lilies look that much more authentic.

STAMENS AND ANTHERS

If you would like to add stamens, they can be done by mixing a yellow, light green, or rusty orange color and piping a few brief dashes to suggest the anthers using a bag with a #3 tip.

DAYLILIES

Use a deep orange with a lighter, yellowish orange, or a medium orange with burnt sienna highlights to make these. Yellow or yellowish-green stamens with deep burnt sienna or reddish-brown anthers look well with these daylilies.

TIGER LILIES

To make these, add little dots (with a #3 tip) of dark brown or a warm black to petals and pipe the petals so that they ripple a bit. For the stamens and anthers you can use shades of yellow-green and/or reddish brown.

STAR GAZER LILIES

Use white and pink, or a deeper cool pink and another cool pale pink shade placed in the same bag to make these. Stamens and anthers can be green or green and burnt sienna. As an optional element for authenticity, you can add little spots of deeper pink to the petals.

YELLOW LILIES

When making, add a yellowish green to the bag, something not too dark or green—try for a color that is a medium, almost lemon yellow. With these lilies, anthers and stamens should be a pale green and a darker warmer green.

Forming Amaryllis

Any two reds, particularly an orangy one and one that includes some burgundy or royal red, can be used together to make an amaryllis. The leaves of these flowers look just like lily leaves.

Mix a warm soft green using yellow and a little purple with not too much blue.

Add to 8 ounces Vanilla Butter Cream (page 133):

4 drops yellow
2 drops purple
4 drops blue

Place some of this alone or with some of another green in a pastry bag fitted with a #59 or #60 tip. Draw leaves onto your cake in long, soft, up-and-down curving strokes. Let some crisscross and overlap.

Forming Irises

The iris is a useful flower to know for cake decorating. Its colors include a beautiful range of blues and purples. Made of interesting strokes of color, irises share with sunflowers the same potential for graphic power. While there are few petals, they can include interesting twists and turns, and can be a very expressive design element.

For a medium blue iris, mix up 2 cups of blue butter cream, a lighter one with 3 to 4 drops of royal blue, and 1 to 3 drops purple, and a darker one using 4 to 6 drops of royal blue and 3 to 7 drops of purple. A yellow color can be mixed up as well. Put some of each blue into a bag with a #60 tip. Use a #350 tip on the bag for the yellow. The end of the iris petal is done either with a short spurt of extra pressure or by going over it a second time (or a bit of both, if you like, for good measure).

Iris leaves are done with a leaf tip such as a #352 or a #45 ribbon tip.

A dusty bluish green—not dark green—is a good color choice for iris leaves, which may add a little variety to the other leaf colors on a cake. Mix some of an existing green into some more butter cream and add a few drops of blue and a drop or two of purple.

Or to 8 ounces Vanilla Butter Cream (page 133) add:

3 drops lemon yellow
2 drops royal blue
1 drop purple

The leaves should be done as straight strokes; try for an angular or sword-like shape.

A SIMPLE FLOWER IN ITS OWN CATEGORY

Forming Violets

Violets are easy to do well. A small, simple, purple flower is a handy design element. You can sneak a few in when you need just a touch of blue or purple or something dark. They are also easy to fashion on the sides of cakes. They are nice in clusters, but also work well sprinkled about. A chocolate cake decorated completely in violets is very pretty, even dainty, but can work as a "masculine" (no pastels, not too many flowers) cake, too. Violets come in other colors such as white, a very pale blue or lavender, and yellow, but the following suggestions are for mixing up a violet violet.

Add to 8 ounces Vanilla Butter Cream (page 133):

Formula #1:

4 to 5 drops royal blue
5 to 7 drops bright purple

Formula #2:

2 to 4 drops bright purple
4 to 7 drops violet

Formula #3:

7 to 8 drops bright purple
4 to 6 drops burgundy
1 to 3 drops violet

For the centers, in another cup, add to 6 ounces Vanilla Butter Cream (page 133):

7 to 10 drops lemon yellow
1 to 2 drops *either:* royal blue, purple, or egg shade

Put the petal color in a pastry bag with a #59 tip and the yellow center color in a bag with a #4 tip. Pipe five small tear-shaped or pear-shaped petals radiating out from a common point. In the center place a simple yellowish dot.

LEAVES FOR VIOLETS

I don't recommend a literal interpretation when doing violet leaves. I make mine rather small, as if the violet were closer to the observer and the leaf in the distance, closer to the "ground." (You'll have to imagine yourself as a rabbit or a squirrel for this to make any sense.) Add some stems here and there using a leaf green color and a #4 tip.

FLOWERS FASHIONED WITH CLUSTERS OF SMALL PETALS

Forming Wisteria

Cascading wisteria can be used to decorate the vertical sides of a cake. There are many possible interpretations of this flower, some more literal and some more fanciful approaches. Shades of lavender, from the very palest to a light or medium purple, and shades of light blue with some violet in them are possible colors.

Try mixing up a very pale blue (add 2 to 3 drops of royal blue or 1 to 2 drops of purple to 8 ounces Vanilla Butter Cream) in one cup. In another cup, mix up a dark lavender to light purple shade (3 to 5 drops violet with 3 to 4 drops of bright purple). In addition, mix up two greens—one should have more yellow and the other more blue; neither color should be too dark. To relate the leaves and flowers it is best if a bit of lavender is used in one or both greens. This type of decoration will function chiefly as a frame for the top of the cake, so I suggest you err on the side of being a bit dull and repetitive. Go for unobtrusive harmony.

Fill two pastry bags fitted with #59 tips a half to two-thirds full with the petal colors. Fill one pastry bag fitted with a #350 or #352 tip with two leaf colors side by side. I like to pipe the leaves first to suggest the pattern of the blossom clusters. Then I fill in the darker petal color blossoms followed by the lighter petals. Finish with a few more small leaves. A suggestion of vines might be added here as well. Use an earth green (not too dark) or a pale brown in a bag with a #3 or #4 tip. Fashion in clusters of very small blossoms; for each blossom, use 1, 2, or 3 petals made up very short downward strokes, angled out slightly.

You can have your vines grow any which way, but I like the clusters (or at least their blossoms) to hang in a perpendicular direction toward the base of the cake. The repetitive direction of the blossoms will suggest a consistent gravitational pull, which will make the flowers appear more lifelike.

Forming Lilacs

Lilacs, like wisteria, can be done any number of ways, so don't hesitate to improvise. The flower of a lilac is made up of small florets, each with either 4 or 8 petals. For cake decorating purposes, it is not necessary to do them with 4- and 8-petaled florets throughout. The florets can be suggested with two to four short strokes using a #59 or #81 tip. Your strokes can be flat or curved. You can also try turning the bag to create a combination of closed circles and crescent shapes.

Beads of butter cream in a darker shade than the rest of the lilac can be used to represent the as-yet-unopened part of the flower. The beads should be piped in clusters at the edge of some of the lilac blooms.

Lavender, purple, and white are the colors most associated with lilacs. There are some interesting blues and pinks as well. A deep reddish purple can serve as a good closed petal color.

For lilac colors, try adding to 8 ounces Vanilla Butter Cream (page 133):

6 to 9 drops bright purple
3 to 5 drops burgundy

Mix 1 to 5 tablespoons of this into a cup of plain Vanilla Butter Cream to make an open petal color. Use green added to white to do the unopened ends of white lilacs. The colors used for wisteria would also make good lilacs.

Use a #59 tip to do petals and #5 tip to do the unopened parts. You may decide to make these somewhat three dimensional. I usually prefer not to make mine too built up, at least not consistently built up all over the cake. Placing lilacs so they cover the edge of your cake and fall onto the side, can add dimension without using tons of butter cream. Highlighting flowers with a lighter shade of florets at the "higher" or fullest part of the lilac will enhance the three-dimensional illusion as well. A few dots of a yellow shade can be piped here and there with a #3 tip to make the centers of some of the florets.

The individual flowers on a lilac bush have a framework like miniature bushes or trees themselves. To suggest this, draw a few twigs to represent the infrastructure in woody green, light brown, or purplish red using a #4 or #5 tip. These can be piped on before, and therefore underneath the blossoms, or integrated throughout. Twigs and light branches can also be piped under the leaves using the same pastry bag with the same color or a paler, browner color. For heavier twigs, pipe more slowly with slightly more pressure.

LEAVES FOR LILACS

Lilac leaves should not be too numerous. Use a soft, yellow green, and make the leaves a bit larger than the leaves you would use for a rose.

Forming Hydrangeas

While I don't suppose hydrangeas are in any way related to lilacs (unless you are fashioning them out of butter cream), I consider them close cousins. Most of the directions for lilacs can be used for hydrangeas as well—with a few exceptions. A lilac flower is shaped more like a bunch of grapes growing upside down. A hydrangea is more like a slightly flattened sphere. The individual florets can be similar, although in most varieties of hydrangea, the florets are made up of larger and flatter petals. The colors for hydrangeas include most of the same shades used for lilacs, but also include pale greens and aqua-blues. These last colors are probably the reason I think hydrangeas need to be included here, however briefly. There are simply not too many flowers one can do in these shades, particularly blue-green.

LEAVES FOR HYDRANGEAS

The edges are slightly serrated, and the leaves are a dark, earthy color. Purple or brown added to a brighter green works.

Here are some other flowers made by piping petals into florets and grouping them in an appropriate shape to create a larger flower:

- geraniums: in bright, orangy red, rose, or pink
- phlox: in pale pinks and lavender
- snowballs: in pale green and white, with or without tiny yellow-green centers
- hyacinths: in white, pink, lavender-blues, and shades of purple

DESIGN ELEMENTS FOR SEASONAL CAKES

Forming Poinsettias

Poinsettia flowers are made with any of the leaf tips (I prefer a #352), which isn't odd, because they are actually leaves that turn a deep bright red when the nights lengthen in December to over 12 hours. The addition of yellow, or yellow-green dots in the center is an important detail.

Mix up a flower color in a red, pink, or greenish white and then mix up a center yellow or yellow-green. You will also need a leaf color. I'd suggest a medium green that's rather bright and not too muddy.

Fill a pastry bag with the flower color. Using the #352 tip, alter the pressure a bit as you move the butter cream through the bag to make the flower. Make anywhere from 4 to 6 petals shaped like leaves radiating out to form the flower. With a #4 tip, pipe yellow in small dots to make a center, and finish with a few leaves of the same size and shape as the leaves of the flower.

Forming Pine Needles and Pine Cones

Pine makes a nice addition to regular leaves in the winter months. Use a variety of greens for this, including very pale and medium blue-greens.

Start by making stems of green or brown piped with a #3 to #5 tip. From these, extend needles of paler or darker green using a #2, #3, or #4 tip. On any one branch all the needles should be the same color and length. If you are creating several branches, you may, of course, want to suggest more than one type of evergreen, by having some branches longer or bluer, or darker, or paler. The needles of white pine can be quite long; for others the needles should run anywhere from ½ to 2½ inches to suggest a bushy Scotch pine.

Pine cones are done in a shade of brown with a #54 or #60 tip and are formed rather like a one-sided zinnia. Make your pine cones one to three times as long as they are wide. Working from the bottom up to the top, pipe the rows of "petals" overlapping one another. If you like, white butter cream can be added between the layers with a #2 tip to suggest snow.

Some Thoughts About Composition

GENERAL ADVICE

I am not too fond of hard and fast rules, particularly in matters of individual taste. So, understand that all the advice offered here is only that, and there are bound to be valid reasons for doing things another way. If your aim is to decorate fluidly in your own style, you are really looking for your own rules. You can begin to develop your own rules by remembering what does and doesn't work for you; imagining what you would like your work to look like; and by seeing in what you have done what you want to do.

Before getting into talking about particular combinations of flowers or colors or set patterns to try, I'll begin with some comments that may be generally helpful.

Absolute *symmetry* is usually not a particularly desirable thing. First of all, it can be boring. Unless your cake (or garden) is the size of Versailles, everything lined up in neat little rows, evenly spaced, will probably end up looking like the planting at a highway rest stop or a municipal parking lot.

Try to *group flowers* together in clusters rather than distributing them evenly around the perimeter (unless you are trying for a wreath effect).

Don't have all your flowers facing the same direction. A dominant *direction* suggests a source of sunlight, but if everything faces one way, it will look as if everything had bloomed together and eliminate the illusion of time passing. Unless you are ambidextrous, you will actually need to work on this. Use your wheel to turn your cake and to get at the surface from different angles.

For the same reason (avoiding what is boring and attempting to evoke the illusion of time), do not make all your flowers of a particular kind the same *size*. Vary the size, the direction, the number of petals (even for those with a "set" number of 6 petals or fewer).

Having a *color scheme* in mind is not a bad thing at all. This usually means limiting the number of colors you will use in a composition rather than using *all* the colors.

However, do try to vary the colors within the group you've chosen. Always try to use more than one shade of any color you are using, such as two or three blues instead of one. Using different *shades* of similar colors adds depth and texture. It creates harmony among colors that might otherwise clash. It also can add to the illusion of the flowers on your cake being in different states of bloom.

Try to have a top and a bottom to your design. This will suggest the existence of gravity and, therefore, place, as opposed to flowers scattered evenly, which suggests wrapping paper. Actually this is a rule often broken to good effect, but it's worth noting nonetheless, particularly if you would like your cake to resemble a garden.

If there is an inscription on your cake, it will indicate which way is up (so to speak), but try to do this even if there isn't an inscription. Allow some air space, particularly in the center and upper half.

Let certain flowers grow up or out from the bottom, and up the sides. You can use the majority of your cake sides for ground or trellis, for flowers and leaves to grow from. Allow some flowers to lean down or fall, as well.

For a round cake without an inscription, one may need to look beyond the obvious to determine what direction your flowers will be "growing." You could consider the center as the open air space and the edges as the lower point or ground level.

Another approach on a large cake (12 inches and up) would be to consider both the center and the edge as "ground level" and to create a ring of air space between them, in other words, place some flowers in the center.

FLORAL DESIGNS

The most requested cakes we do are mixed florals. When you do a mixed floral cake, choose three or four flowers to start off. Try to choose flowers that provide some variation in shape or texture—roses, tulips, and black-eyed Susans, for example; or lilacs, roses, and peonies. Don't try to do everything on one cake. How many different families of color you choose to work with should depend somewhat on the size of your cake. The smaller the cake, the more likely it will look better without too many completely different colors. On cakes 10 inches and up, there should probably be more variety. Flowers all done in shades of a single color can look elegant on a 7-inch cake, but rather dull on an 11-inch one.

If you have your heart set on a riot of color, try to incorporate at least two shades of any color you do use, three is usually better still.

Begin by mixing up 2 or 3 cups of colored butter cream in the colors you plan on using the most of. These will be your dominant colors. Next, mix up at least two greens to go with them. Look at these colors in their cups to determine if they go well together. It's easier to make changes now than when they are on your cake.

Mentally divide your cake into different areas of flower activity. Of course, size will certainly come into this equation. How many large and small areas will determine the look of your cake? These areas can overlap into one another and/or appear to end behind, or in front of, one another. Working with an uneven number of, say, rose patches, can prevent cakes from becoming too symmetrical.

On an 8-inch cake, I would probably have roses in two or three areas, one of those areas being larger (with more roses) than the others; irises in two or three places; one place for daisies; a few violets in the different areas and on the sides. I might put a few peonies or another round, multipetaled flower in with my roses. Wisteria or lilacs might be in four or five places on the sides. Look for patterns yourself in the cakes illustrated in the color section of this book.

Another popular choice for floral cakes is to do the whole cake in one or two flowers. Cake size is important in determining the suitability of certain flowers. Generally, the smaller flowers look best alone on smaller cakes. The larger the flower, the more suitable it is to be the lone decoration on a larger cake. A 6- or 7-inch cake done with just violets is quite pretty. At 10 inches it is more likely to look homely. (And it goes without saying that if you are just getting the knack of doing a particular flower, decorating a whole cake with that one flower probably isn't the best idea.)

Cakes 7 to 9 inches covered with white daisies with yellow centers (popular for showers) are nice, but 10 inches is pushing it in my book. Irises and sunflowers would be among my choices for cakes 10 inches and up. A flower we do on a very small scale would be tulips. For the most part, they are better alone on a cake smaller than 10 inches.

On cakes 9 inches and larger, consider adding a secondary flower, particularly if the dominant flower isn't large. Roses with a sprinkling of violets would be one combination; daisies with black-eyed Susans, another.

If you *are* doing a cake that is basically decorated with one flower, (and you are familiar enough with that flower) it is nice to include a little extra detail, such as stems or branches. You might throw in some thorns or a few rose hips, for instance, on a rose cake. Add your best tulip leaves on an all-tulip cake.

Try to provide enough variety in the color family you are using to keep it interesting. And if you are doing an all-sunflower cake, don't have the sunflowers all staring up at you, all the same size. If it's all lilacs, try to put three or four different varieties on your cake.

Flying in the face of this edict is the all-white-on-white, or all-chocolate-on-chocolate cake. While it can be fun to do these in different shades of chocolate, or shades of white, these are cakes where color is not the main thing. They do provide an opportunity for you to be very aware of all the possible texture variations, and to show off the shapes of leaves and flowers. With a colorless cake you can use a greater number of different flowers, as you needn't worry so much about your cake being too busy.

A word about decorating with chocolate frosting: You must add your chocolate when it is still warm enough to blend completely. Otherwise it can form little lumps of chocolate later inside your decorating tips. Therefore, when you first blend your chocolate butter cream, it may be too soft to decorate with. Wait a bit. Chocolate adds some extra body to butter cream, and is actually a little easier to use than the vanilla stuff when it is at the right temperature.

Picture Cakes

Somewhere, I've seen it written that the Cupcake Café prides itself on being able to put anything on a cake. I think I would amend that to say that we have the *chutzpa* (or lack of common sense) to try to put anything anyone asks for on a cake. This, and the fact that butter cream makes great paint, is the real secret to our picture cakes, and it can be yours as well.

The idea of "anything" on a cake may sound daunting to some people, though I hope to others it sounds liberating. I'll start by talking about ideas for children's cakes since cakes for children constitute the majority of our "picture cakes."

DECIDING WHAT TO PUT ON A CHILDREN'S CAKE

Cartoon and comic book characters are, of course, popular choices for kids, and some adults as well. If you go this route, and you haven't done it before, try to choose the least complicated acceptable choice. (In other words, wait awhile before you promise a six-year-old you'll put "anything" he asks for on his cake.) Simple is always better. It isn't just easier, it looks better, too. And don't be afraid to simplify a complex element, such as a realistic face. Children are good with symbols. If a super hero or heroine is wearing the right costume, they'll know who it is.

Consider characters from picture books for possible cake designs, as well as the animated ones. "Madeline," "Babar," and "Curious George" all make particularly attractive cakes. The colors are appealing, the pictures are both simple and relaxed, making them effective and easy to do. Obviously, there are plenty of other possibilities, and a child's favorite book would be the best choice. Some others that are a little harder but are still recommended for copying would be: Ernest Shepard's illustrations for *Winnie-the-Pooh*; Arnold Lobel's *Frog and Toad*; Margaret Wise Brown's *Good Night Moon*, and her *The Runaway Bunny*; or anything by *The Cat in the Hat* author, Dr. Seuss. Not recommended for real beginners is Beatrix

Potter's *Peter Rabbit,* although it is a popular choice for the slightly ambitious. Maurice Sendak's *Where the Wild Things Are* has been used to make some nifty cakes. "Spot" is a fine choice for the very young.

SOME OTHER THEMES, PLACES, AND ANIMALS THAT ARE FUN TO DO ON A CAKE

(starting with the fairly simple and moving to the more difficult)

Rainbows

Outer space with planets
    and rockets

Ladybugs

Dinosaurs (with and without
    prehistoric volcanoes in the
    background)

Alligators

Dragonflies

Butterflies

Underwater scenes (including
    tropical fish, whales, sharks,
    mermaids, and octopi)

Frogs and lizards

Dragons

Unicorns

Monsters

Jungle animals

Circus scenes

Baseball, soccer, basketball, and
    hockey games

Castles, knights

Pirate ships

The younger the child, the simpler you should make your design. A favorite toy or doll is another thing you might consider putting on a very young child's cake. Some of our most interesting cakes for children have been those decorated with a copy of an original drawing done by the child. Allowing a child to really design his or her own cake is one of the nicest tributes you could put on a cake.

SUBJECTS FOR ADULT PICTURE CAKES

You can, of course, put anything you like on a picture cake that is not for a child, but here's some general advice:

Whatever subject you pick, try to choose something you have some personal connection with. All other things being equal, try to copy pictures for which you feel some enthusiasm; don't stick yourself with a subject you can't visualize to save your life. (There's bound to be another subject that would work for that person just as well.)

Pictures of real people are not recommended unless you can really paint or are really able to do caricatures. If you can paint or do caricatures, then fine. Just leave yourself enough time, and remember that what you put on a cake you can take off.

MAKING PICTURES ON CAKES

After you've chosen a "theme," you'll need to collect any reference material you'll be using. (Unless you are able to work strictly from memory or your imagination.) This might be an object with Mickey Mouse on it, a child's toy, a comic or a picture book, an old ballpark program, a nature magazine, or a dinosaur book.

Next, you'll want to design your cake on paper. Start by tracing a cake circle, board, or cake pan, the size of your cake onto paper so you'll have an accurate idea of how much room you have to work with. If you are going to be copying all or part of your design from another source, you don't have to make a drawing with a lot of detail. You just want to determine what is going where. Remember, even a fine line piped in butter cream is much heftier than a line drawn in pen or pencil. Don't plan on attempting a lot of small-scale details. As I've said, kids are quite good at interpreting symbols.

I recommend you begin any picture cake, adult or child, by laying out the background first. Choose to work over vanilla if possible, unless you are creating a night or outer space scene.

When you mix up colors for the *background*, try to keep them light and on the clear side. Avoid murky colors and using too many colors to begin with. Whatever colors you are using, go a shade lighter to start. For a jungle or forest, for instance, try yellow and pale green. For sky, use a very pale clear royal, or "true" blue; for water, a clear bright aqua. Spread the colored butter cream over your cake on the appropriate areas and smooth over with a large spatula.

Over this you can *sketch your design* out using black or brown butter cream in a pastry bag with a comfortable writing tip such as a #3. When you've done this you can fill in your design with colored frosting using a #3, #4, or #5 tip, depending on the scale of the work. A small tapered spatula can be used to smooth over some areas of color if you wish, or instead you may choose to work with the butter cream to enhance the texture of your picture.

For creating *scales* (on fish and mermaids and dragons) and *feathers* (for that big yellow bird) #352 tip is good. A #16 tip makes a good *hairy* "Cookie Monster" or "Elmo."

Another method, which some people prefer, is to draw their design on the cake using no butter cream at all. You can engrave, or scratch the surface or background with a #2 tip or a bamboo skewer. This drawing is then filled in with different shades of colored butter cream. Lines and smaller details are piped on last.

People who paint and others may feel more comfortable working in larger areas of color adding the smaller ones and the lines as they go, rather than drawing lines and then coloring them in.

Some people prefer to add the background last. Do whatever feels most comfortable. Creating picture cakes is very much like painting in butter cream, and there can be as many ways of handling the medium as there are ways to paint. But keep in mind: Cakes are for eating, not for hanging on the wall, try to enjoy what you're doing.

Inscriptions on picture cakes are usually added last, on top of the background. Around the perimeter of the cake is another good place to put your inscription, rather than in the center of your design. Printing is often preferable to writing in script since it is easier to read in a curved layout. For your inscription, use a color that will stand out enough so you can read it, but not so much that it distracts from your picture. Red is often a good choice. It is legible against most backgrounds and not too light or dark.

Wedding Cakes

Obviously, a great many wedding cakes are not frosted in butter cream. We are only dealing here with the sort we do at the Café, that is, cakes frosted and decorated in butter cream. After reading about how to put together multitiered cakes we can address the fun part, decorating. But first, an important word of advice to first-time multitiered cake builders. *Give yourself enough time.* You will need time to plan your design, frost all the tiers, and assemble them (which may entail a trip to the hardware store to buy dowels or time to find that coping saw). You may also need to allow extra time for baking if your oven isn't large enough to accommodate all the necessary cake pans at one time—or if one of your pans is needed for double duty. You may also need to make more than one batch of cake batter and/or butter cream as well. And, of course, all the layers of cake will need to cool before you begin assembling them.

What this comes down to then is: When preparing tiered cakes it is a good idea to do your baking and frosting a day ahead, and, in any event, leave yourself enough time.

HOW TO PUT TOGETHER MULTITIERED CAKES

With all wedding cakes and other multitiered cakes, take extra care when frosting each tier. They should all be as cylindrical as possible. Try not to have your layers slant too much. They should be as level as possible. If you need to trim cake off the top with a knife to achieve this, do so. You want the sides to appear straight up and down. If the surface texture is meant to be fairly smooth, it should not look distressed. You may wish to frost and chill your cake, remove excess frosting, then frost it again, repeating this a couple of times if necessary.

If a wedding cake is to be more than one tier, frost all the tiers individually first. You will need a Masonite circle for each tier, the same size as the cake pans you have used. You will also need another board at least 2 inches larger than the bottom layer to hold the whole thing.

Most cake plates are too small and are awkward for moving a cake around or taking it in and out of the refrigerator. You will also need several ¼- or ⅜-inch-thick dowels.

After you have finished frosting the bottom tier of your cake, center it on your cake board. Insert one dowel straight up and down into the cake at the highest point in your cake (though of course we hope it is level and there is no highest point). Mark the point at which it emerges from the cake. Take the dowel out carefully and clamp it down, cutting off the extra length with a small hand saw such as a coping saw. Now cut three to five more pieces the same size as this first piece—three more pieces if you are supporting a 4- to 7-inch cake; five more if your next layer is 10 inches or larger. The next tier will be resting on these pieces of wood, so it is imperative that they all be the same height, whether your first tier is truly level or not. So please, please, cut them all exactly the same size! (And if you mess up, cut a new piece, or take off the extra length as needed.)

Carefully center a cake circle the same size as the next tier on top of the bottom tier. There should be an equal amount of space all around the perimeter if it is centered properly. (For example a 10-inch circle centered on a 14-inch cake will leave a 2-inch border of uncovered cake all around it.) Check to make sure before proceeding.

Lightly trace the position of the cake circle and then remove it. Insert your cut dowels as straight up and down as you can into the bottom tier of cake, ½ to 1 inch inside this circle in an evenly spaced circular pattern. Place a few tablespoons of butter cream inside this circle and center your next tier on the bottom tier over the dowels.

You now have a two-tiered cake! If you are making a three-tiered cake you would repeat this process for the next tier, with fewer dowels as the size of your layer dictates. Always use at least four, not necessarily for support, but to help keep everything level.

If you are using a "cake topper" such as a bride and groom figurine, you may want a dowel or two inserted beneath a small circle on the top tier as well. I recommend this if the figures are relatively heavy—such as the ceramic variety—so they don't sink into the cake. (Plastic figures probably won't need a platform to stand on.) You can cover this top circle with frosting if necessary, although your circle need not be any larger than the "topper" itself.

To close in any space between the tiers, pipe butter cream with a star tip (such as a #16 or #21), and smooth it out with a fingertip.

The base of each tier may be embellished if you wish before putting on other decorations, and you may wish to embellish the edges as well.

A #16 tip can be used to make a border of shells along the base of each tier.

A #45 tip can be used to create a flat or wavy ribbon.

A #4 or #5 tip can be used to make small beads of butter cream piped to line up close together like a string of small pearls.

Guide to Tiered-Cake Sizes

The following is a rough guide to how much cake you will need for how many people.

NUMBER OF PEOPLE	NUMBER OF TIERS	SIZE OF LAYERS
up to 20 to 25	2	8″ + 4″
up to 30 to 35	2	9″ (or 10″) + 6″
40 to 45	2	11″ + 7″
50 to 60	3*	12″ + 8″ + 4″
up to 75	3	12″ + 9″ + 6″
80 to 90	3	13″ + 9″ + 6″ (or 5″)
100	3	14″ + 10″ + 6″
150	3	16″ + 12″ + 8″

*The third tier in this case is optional, suggested for aesthetic purposes.

A wedding cake should be fun for all parties concerned. Although this may seem glib—and despite a fair amount of experience to the contrary—I still think it is at least an ideal to work toward. Decorating a wedding cake can, indeed, be fun, and it is much more likely to be so if you can be relaxed about it. This is one cake you really want to plan—not only because of the amount of attention that is likely to be paid to it, but also because a multitiered cake takes a while to decorate, and having a plan or design will make it that much easier, quicker, and more enjoyable to get the work done.

When planning your design, keep in mind that the vertical sides of wedding cakes are visually as important, if not more important, than the top of each tier. The sides, in fact, constitute the greater area of exposed decorating space. A wedding cake is, then, essentially a vertical composition, so design accordingly. Unless you are decorating your own wedding cake (which seems like a rather insane thing to do), your design should be something of a collaboration with the bride and groom. Be careful, though, not to agree to do something impossible, or something you find disagreeable. Be sure you are working with flowers (or other compositional elements) with which you feel comfortable and confident. Simple is often better.

The white-on-white wedding cake is not dead and gone, but it has a lot of colorful company. I have made white-on-white cakes, and plenty of pastel, "pale, pale" cakes, and "whisper peach," ecru, champagne, and ivory cakes with a touch of this or that. However, we get at least as many requests for wedding cakes festooned with butter cream flowers in jewel tones, autumn colors, leaves, grapes, sunflowers, wild flowers, poppies, and all shades of blue—in short any and every kind of flower and color scheme.

Besides flowers, we've done wedding cakes with skyscrapers, Venetian palaces, and a Coney Island roller coaster. We've done wedding cakes topped with antique bride and groom figurines, the owl and the pussy cat and their pea green boat, mice, Daisy and Donald Duck, and at least one wind-up Godzilla. By now you should be singing "Anything Goes." Keep this in mind, although I will offer below some design suggestions, which I hope you will think of as no more than stepping-off points for your own designs:

1. On each tier pipe white roses only. Use dark green and reddish leaves and a few branches. On the bottom of each tier pipe a ribbon border.

2. Use different shades of red roses and chrysanthemums on each tier, with oak leaves and hydrangeas in shades of pale to medium blue, blue-green, and violet.

3. Pipe roses of pale peach and yellow together with white and pale green lilacs and grapes or elderberry.

4. Use autumn-colored wildflowers, chrysanthemums, and sunflowers with autumn leaves and branches of bittersweet.

5. On the sides, pipe spring bulbs such as tulips and iris. On the tops of the tiers use peonies in shades of dark pink and violet, and roses in pale pink and white.

6. Use all blue flowers such as iris, blue flag, morning glories, violets, delphiniums, and forget-me-nots, with a green vine such as ivy.

Let your imagination range free.

Index